BREAK FREE FROM
NARCISSISTIC
MOTHERS

BREAK FREE FROM NARCISSISTIC MOTHERS

A Step-by-Step Workbook for Ending Toxic Behavior, Setting Boundaries, and Reclaiming Your Life

Hannah Alderete, LMHC

ULYSSES PRESS

Published by:
Ulysses Press
PO Box 3440
Berkeley, CA 94703
www.ulyssespress.com

ISBN: 978-1-64604-255-5
Library of Congress Catalog Number: 2021937734

Printed in the United States by Kingery Printing Company
10 9 8 7 6 5 4 3 2 1

Acquisitions editor: Claire Sielaff
Managing editor: Claire Chun
Project manager: Renee Rutledge
Editor: Ariel Adams
Proofreader: Beret Olsen
Front cover design: Rebecca Lown
Interior design: what!design @ whatweb.com
Production: Jake Flaherty, Yesenia Garcia-Lopez

To my kin: G, K, and M.

Contents

Chapter 1

WHY YOU'RE HERE

"I think I'm finally coming to terms with the fact that my mom may be a narcissist," said Mel in our first therapy session. A creative and flamboyant woman in her early forties with curly red hair and tattoos lining her arms, Mel had sought me out after an aha moment last spring, in which she could no longer deny the reality of her mother.

"Honestly, I think I always knew, but something about this last round of spending time with her really jolted me awake." Mel told her mom that after five years of tirelessly working at her art gallery job as an assistant, she was finally recognized for her hard work and received the promotion of her dreams: to chief curator. Instead of giving her the hugs, praise, and celebration she had hoped for (but deep down knew she wouldn't get), her mother simply looked at her and said, "That's nice, honey, but I really can't hear about this right now. I've got a headache," and walked off to her room, where she proceeded to lie down for a nap. Stunned, Mel walked out of her mother's home, got into her car, and just sat. She was swirling with all kinds of emotions—rage, sadness, disappointment, shock—and yet felt as if the clouds had parted and she could finally see her mother for who she was: a narcissist.

When Mel and I explored her story further, we found countless times when her mother shamed Mel for an emotion, criticized her very normal needs as "selfish," and batted away Mel's boundaries as if they were made of gossamer. Examples of her mother's lack of caring ranged from, "Do you really think you're good enough to sing?" to "I don't have time to listen to you cry," suggesting that Mel's feelings were an imposition. Through repeated experiences like the ones above, Mel never got the sense that she *mattered* to her mother. Nor did she feel that her mother ever really knew her, which is a common experience shared among adult daughters of narcissistic mothers.

Mel noted that this revelation of her mother's narcissism was a long time coming, but what kept her from fully seeing the truth were the unhelpful beliefs she had taken in regarding mothers and daughters. "I always felt that I *should* love my mom unconditionally, that that's what good daughters do, you know? I never got the sense that I was allowed to even consider what I needed in the relationship. For most of my life, my relationship with my mom was one where she mattered more than I did, and I could never just be her daughter that *she* loved unconditionally. There were countless conditions I had to follow just to get the bare minimum."

Other adult daughters of narcissistic mothers have shared very similar beliefs they've unconsciously bought into about mother-daughter relationships. Ellen, a 29-year-old pharmacist, told me once, "It never occurred to me that my mom was being abusive and controlling until I started talking about it." Ellen, like many adult daughters, learned early on to adapt to her mother's emotional insensitivity, neglect, and childlike tantrums. Over time, these adaptations became repeated behaviors that consistently put her mother's needs above her own.

When she awoke from this trance-like adherence to the often-toxic message that "family is family no matter what," it was as if someone had finally turned on the light and she saw what she had been living in. She shared, "It was one of those beautiful autumn days where the sky is neon blue and the sun's warmth feels like you're wearing a weighted blanket. I was driving over to my mom's house and all of the sudden I felt cold, as if a giant had blotted out the sun. My stomach got fluttery and cramped, and I thought I was going to be sick. When I pulled over to catch my breath and figure out what was happening, I realized that I was having a panic attack about seeing my mom. I was afraid that she was going to ruin this beautiful day with another one of her 'episodes' where she basically rips apart my life choices in some form or another."

Ellen realized that she could no longer pretend that her relationship with her mom was "fine" or "just mom being mom." Some dormant part in her began to awaken to the truth of what was happening. This healthy part of Ellen nudged her out of the belief system that was veiling the truth about her mother and finally helped her recognize the reality that something would need to change. That something would not be her mother, and this was when she knew she needed tools to support her own transformation.

Your story may not look exactly like Mel's or Ellen's, but you're in their experiences. They are you: a woman who is coming to grips with the reality of her mother. Whether you're just now realizing that your mother may be a narcissist, or have known your whole life and are no longer in contact, I hope to offer you a place in which you can be held, validated, and supported in your journey back to your *self*. We cannot give you a new mother, but we can give you a new relationship to all the parts of you that had to live underground during your formative years, and welcome them back home.

The Emphasis of the Book

This book is dedicated to you and to reality. We need both in order to take you out of the fantasy that narcissistic mothers live in and to bring you back into the truth of your feelings, needs, identity, boundaries, and aspirations. According to the *Oxford Dictionary*, reality can be defined as "the world or the state of things as they actually exist, as opposed to an idealistic or notional idea of them." One of the main driving forces that keeps narcissism alive is fantasy. Narcissists are masterful actors who need to believe in fantasy so that they don't collapse under the weight of reality, a defense mechanism stemming from their own traumatic childhoods. Narcissists need other people in their lives. Without others, they have no way to define themselves. A narcissist does not have a sense of self, which means that their "self supply" comes from everyone around them. Your mother needed you to help her maintain her fantasy and, in using you this way, subjected you to treatment that left you feeling confused and in doubt about your reality. You've had to constrict yourself, shrink your needs, and deftly maneuver around your mother in ways that perpetuated more pain in your life. Being raised by a narcissist causes significant deficits both in one's self-perception and one's beliefs about the world.

As a child, you took in the belief that your needs pale in comparison to your mother's. Julie Hall, author of *The Narcissist in Your Life: Recognizing the Patterns and Learning to Break Free*, an expert in narcissistic abuse whose ideas will be shared in this book, puts it this way, "The fundamental experience of children in the narcissistic home is not being seen."[1] Children *need* to be seen and heard. Psychologists call this *attunement*, which is the ability of the mother/father/caregiver to be responsive to a child's needs. There is a word for children who have been chronically unseen. It's called trauma. Gabor Maté, a mind-body physician and trauma expert, defines the essence of trauma as "[the] disconnection from ourselves. Trauma is not terrible things that happen from the other side—those are

---

1. Julie L. Hall, *The Narcissist in Your Life: Recognizing the Patterns and Learning to Break Free* (New York: Da Capo Lifelong Books, 2019), 63.

traumatic. But the trauma is that very separation from the body and emotions. So the real question is, 'How did we get separated and how do we reconnect?'"[2]

Maté's last question is where we will put some of our focus: How do we reconnect? We do this by turning toward our own needs and learning the language of our emotions, so that we can use them adaptively. Through the practice of self-attunement comes responsibility, which means "ability to respond." It's one thing to know what you feel; it's quite another to respond to your feelings adequately. Your mother taught you to ignore yourself, so it will feel quite unnatural to begin this process. However, anything that is learned can be unlearned, so take comfort in this! How would you respond to your own child, or to a child you care for, who is learning something for the first time? They may struggle, feel like giving up, cry, be confused, or feel deeply frustrated. How would you hold space for this little one to have their feelings, while helping them stay with what they're learning? Can you direct this same response back to yourself?

So much of the work you will be doing will help your own inner child feel seen, supported, and safe. You are starting from a very young place within yourself. Treat that space with care and consideration. There is no rushing, pushing, bullying, or harassing allowed in this space. Only that which a child can grow from: nurturance, understanding, compassion, healthy limits, and plenty of room to make mistakes. You are entitled to this space for learning, growing, and *messing up*. In fact, I would encourage you to lean into imperfection and see it as a natural space that we all inhabit. None of us is ever going to be perfect and we aren't always going to get things right. *And that's okay*. I would like to invite you, as you do this work, to view yourself with as little judgment as possible. You likely internalized a lot of judgment. However, there is an antidote to judgment, and it's called self-compassion, which is the ability to register and care for the part of us experiencing pain.

In many ways, you were your mother's receptacle where she could dispose of her own unwanted feelings and negative self-beliefs. Any time your reality threatened her fantasy, you would pay the price. That might have looked like being shamed, accused, gaslit, judged, ridiculed, or ignored, all of which played a role in how you developed your sense of self and identity. However, if you did well at something—playing, unbeknownst to you, into her fantasy of the perfect family, perfect daughter—she took ownership of your success.[3] As much as you attempted to build your own sense of self, which was your birthright, there was always a fissure in this process. Daughters who experience emotional whiplash from their mothers typically develop into people pleasers and perfectionists, roles that began as

---

2. Jeanara Nerenberg, "Why Are So Many Adults Today Haunted by Trauma?" *Greater Good Magazine,* last modified June 8, 2017, https://greatergood.berkeley.edu/article/item/why_are_so_many_adults_today_haunted_by_trauma.

3. Hall, *The Narcissist in Your Life,* 31.

attempts to regulate their mothers' changing moods. Underlying the people-pleaser façade is the fear of other people's feelings toward you. When you take on a pleaser role, you have learned that the safest route is the one where the other person stays defined, not you. This means denying parts of yourself and living a half-life, so to speak. Paralleling the role of people pleaser is the impostor syndrome. This can be categorized as a fear that you do not really belong, and that others will eventually find this out. What people-pleasing and impostor syndrome have in common is the sense that who you are is not enough. Underlying this belief is another one: others cannot be trusted, nor can you trust yourself. If you can relate, I hope in this moment you can begin to feel some compassion for yourself and register the magnitude of what you've internalized.

Given that narcissistic mothers live in a fantasy, you and I are going to practice seeing through it and anchoring back into reality. I've heard countless stories of adult daughters who have been told by well-meaning, albeit ignorant, friends and family members to ignore the reality of their narcissist mother. To outsiders, she may look nonthreatening, but that is because she plays her part well. When an adult daughter begins to practice setting boundaries with her mother, these well-meaning yet ignorant individuals misinterpret this as being uncaring. I hear reports of outsiders saying things like, "She can't be all bad," "Why don't you try seeing it from her perspective?" or my favorite, "Are you sure that's what she did/said?" *These individuals will never know what you know. But the truth is, they don't need to in order for your experiences to be valid.* You don't need to see things from her perspective either because, truthfully, that's an impossibility. Nor would it be healthy for you to try to do so. What we can do, however, is help you see things from *your* perspective. It is from this place that real change can emerge.

What I'd like to offer you is something deeper than simply understanding narcissism, though that is something we will cover. I'd like to offer you a new kind of relationship to your *self*. One in which your feelings can be honored, listened to, and treated as important information to make decisions from. A place where your needs are not only acknowledged, but responded to. In narcissistic abuse, among the primary aspects of self that get threatened are *emotions* and *needs*. In fact, these two life forces start to feel very endangered, taking such a significant backseat that they may become erased from awareness.

Throughout the book, you will see a lot of referring back to what you feel and need. The reason behind this is rooted in the belief that our feelings and needs are fundamental to who we are. Without our feelings, we would be lost. When our emotions or needs have been routinely ignored, minimized, or neglected by significant others, it teaches us to do the same. When we put our energy into escaping our feelings and needs, we end up experiencing more pain. For instance, can you imagine what would happen if you ignored your fear?

In some circles, striving to be fearless is considered a sign of strength, but I would highly disagree. We need our fear to alert us to danger, just like we need *all* of our emotions to keep us healthy. We cannot live functional lives if we are running around without access to what we feel or need.

Along the way, you'll meet many other women who share your experiences in some form or another. (The women mentioned in the book are composites of individuals with whom I've worked over the years. All names, identities, and details have been disguised and altered to maintain confidentiality.) These women will guide you through the chapters as they tell their stories, and you'll be invited to stay connected to your own. You likely have some outdated belief systems that no longer require your adherence, and it will be vital that you create new ones so that you can live with more freedom.

This book is about helping you *step into your truth*. We will be doing some digging to help you unearth the parts of yourself that had to go underground in order for you to survive. The path toward welcoming these parts back into being always comes back to the body, which is where our emotions come through. Learning to tune into your body will allow for a deeper self-awareness to emerge. Paying attention to yourself in this way takes practice, patience, and a lot of compassion. When you can have a relationship to your body, you also form a relationship to your feelings, which serve to enhance your life, even when they're painful. Your feelings only want to serve you. When all feelings can be seen as purposeful energies that have something to say, then there's no need to be at war with them.

What We Won't Encourage

I'd like to share a few things about what this book will not be encouraging or suggesting. This book will not be about finding ways to manage your mother. You will not be instructed to over-function for her or self-sacrifice to "keep the peace." Nor will you be taught how to be a "better listener" to your narcissistic mother, offer premature forgiveness, or do anything that puts you back in a self-denying role. You are not responsible for your mother's feelings or needs.

If you are looking to make peace with your mother through forgiveness in some form, I strongly encourage you to work with a therapist trained in narcissistic abuse who can help you do this safely. I know many adult daughters who have been unfortunately advised to forgive their mothers, which led them deeper down the rabbit hole instead of out. While some daughters may get to that point, many don't, and it is vital that this be normalized. Forgiveness is not required for you to recover.

We will, of course, cover ways to set authentic boundaries with your mother, which will necessitate communicating with her, but always coming back to yourself, asking, "how am I feeling about this? What do I need in this moment?" If the answer is "no contact," "I don't like this," "I want out," "this doesn't feel good," "I'm not feeling safe," then my hope is that you will heed that call and make taking care of yourself a priority in that moment.

This book will not be about empowering you to bash your mother or engage in mother-blaming either. While you may truly hate her and *want* to bash her, it won't offer you relief in the end. I do want to encourage you to work with a therapist who can help you process the deeper feelings that may come up as you do this kind of trauma recovery. The aim of this book is about knowing *you*. Specifically, I want to invite your subjective experiences to have a seat at the table without needing to justify or minimize their existence. Along with honoring your subjectivity, we'll also take a clinical look at what narcissism is, so that you can have more freedom to relate to it with objectivity.

Julie Hall, whose work I've previously mentioned, makes an important note about children in narcissistic homes. She states, "Children in narcissistic families learn to meet their parents' needs while burying their own. They learn that to survive they must constantly work to read their parents' emotions while masking or faking theirs."[4] It doesn't matter if your childhood looked "normal" or even felt normal most of the time; you can still experience trauma under an idyllic roof. Trauma is not limited to overt acts such as physical violence, war, or sexual abuse. Traumatic experiences can be small, insidious, and covert, which makes calling them out difficult, since they cannot be seen in the most obvious of ways.

Emotional abuse, covert incest, gaslighting, unhealthy boundaries, and narcissism itself, are examples of unseen trauma. These traumatic experiences lead to a dysregulated nervous system much in the same way that overt physical trauma does. Adult children of narcissists who are grappling with their own trauma, attempting to put the pieces of the puzzle together, will often find themselves wondering if they even "had it that bad?" The reason for this doubt is partially due to the fact that being raised by a narcissist trains you to question reality, and narcissists don't always present in the most obvious of ways. Many of the women I've worked with have described their mothers to be like Jekyll and Hyde, never knowing which version they would get. In one instance, their mothers are disavowing them, telling them how worthless they are, and in another offering affection and praise. Narcissists cannot see their own narcissism. Many, in fact, would describe themselves as upstanding citizens who only want the best for their children. They may even go so far as to say they would do anything for their children, which to them feels like the truth. The children, on the other hand, experience something very different.

---

4. Hall, *The Narcissist in Your Life*, 73.

If you find yourself questioning your experience, wondering if you're just making it up, consider this a symptom of narcissistic abuse. Many adult children of narcissists will find themselves questioning the reality of their experiences, sometimes for years. The "was it really that bad?" question comes up a lot in therapy, and I always like to remind adult daughters that yes, it was that bad, but it wasn't that obvious. You may not be able to directly point to one solid example of abuse, because in some cases, the abusive behavior was designed to keep you from seeing it. As children, we have no real choice but to believe what our parents tell us. If they say they didn't do something, even though our experience tells us something else, we default to their reality in place of our own. If a child's mind could talk, it might sound like, "My mom wouldn't lie to me. She is the adult, after all. There must be something wrong with me, my memory is faulty, my feelings are wrong and inappropriate. I must have done something to deserve this."

What may be helpful for you to keep in mind in your recovery is the recognition that you've been living under the influence of an individual who cannot perceive reality correctly. In some ways, it's the equivalent of following the whims of a five-year-old who cannot perceive anything outside of herself. While you may understand this intellectually, it's important to keep reminding yourself of this fact so that you can start to challenge the unhealthy beliefs you took in. At the beginning, this may feel like a tug of war between the part of you that can logically comprehend that you took in a false narrative and the part of you that has been conditioned to deny it.

I'd like for you to take a minute and reflect on some questions below. You can do this in the space below or in a journal, or think the answers to yourself. Do whatever feels right in this moment.

What are your hopes for yourself as you read this book?

BREAK FREE FROM NARCISSISTIC MOTHERS

If you could name the most toxic message that you'd like to overcome, what would it be?

How might your life look different if this toxic message weren't dominating your thoughts and perceptions?

What are you willing to risk, change, and endure in order to live the life you most desire for yourself?

_____

_____

_____

_____

_____

_____

Now, I'd like to encourage you to reflect on where you've been in your life, where you are now, and what you want for your future self. Let this be free flowing, unrestricted, and full of your clearest wishes and intentions.

As you embark on recovering, it's important that you take a holistic perspective that accounts for all parts of yourself and your life. In some ways it's like planting a garden. We don't simply throw a seed into the ground and hope for the best. If you want your garden to bloom and grow, you've got to tend the soil, make sure it gets the right amount of water and sunlight, and, of course, check and see how it's doing every day. Perhaps you do some weeding to make sure the garden doesn't get overrun. You get the idea. As you think of yourself holistically, you may discover some aspects that get more attention than others. This is neither good nor bad, just something to notice.

Below are a few things I believe are important for anyone recovering from psychological and emotional abuse to implement and practice.

Take Up More Space: This book is dedicated to your growth and self-discovery, so the first order of business is learning how to take up more space, both physically and emotionally. Journaling is a wonderful tool to safely express your emotions, where they can be exactly as they are: real and free to exist. If you live in close quarters with others, please secure a place and time for yourself to simply be alone with your thoughts and feelings. If that is hard to come by, there are creative options to try out: Find a room that's comfortable for you, put your headphones on, play relaxing music, and let yourself journal. If you're able, find a place in nature and take in its healing properties. Give yourself plenty of breaks and moments of self-care if emotions start to run high and you feel overwhelmed with the process.

Find a Therapist to Work With: Anytime we're doing a deep dive into our family dynamics, emotional experiences, and traumatic memories, it's nonnegotiable that we seek out professional help with a therapist. Working through narcissistic abuse should be done with the help of a therapist who has experience treating this population. If therapy is difficult for you to afford, there are plenty of therapists who work on a sliding scale to meet financial needs.

If you cannot find a therapist who specializes in narcissistic abuse, I would encourage you to start with a clinician who is trauma-informed. Please note that if your therapist begins to suggest that you try seeing things from your mother's perspective, pushes forgiveness, downplays the narcissism, or brushes past your experiences, it may be time to look elsewhere. Some questions to ask a prospective therapist might look like:

- What is your understanding of narcissism? Have you treated folks who have experienced narcissistic abuse?

- Tell me about your orientation toward trauma recovery. How do you work with folks who have been emotionally abused?

Have a Supportive Person or Group to Be With: A supportive person can include a spouse, partner, friend, sibling, family member, or close colleague. Having a person that you can safely lean on during times of stress (and even joy) is so essential. However, please refrain from confiding in your children or attempting to reach out to your mother for soothing. These two categories are off-limits. A supportive person is someone you can express your feelings to and spend quality time with. You should feel safe and comfortable with this person. Joining a group whose aim is to recover from narcissistic abuse, trauma, or codependency is also a wonderful way to build community and connection.

Rest: Your nervous system will likely be activated to some degree doing this work. Some of the daughters I've worked with really struggle to slow down and rest, a symptom of over-giving to their narcissistic mothers. Rest is as important as setting aside time to exercise, meditate, connect with others, and spend time alone. I would suggest 20 minutes per day of simply *resting*, i.e., no phone scrolling, reading the news, watching tv, etc., as a good place to start. If meditating is something you find restful, utilize that practice as well.

Time in Nature: Another beautiful practice for regulating the nervous system is being out in nature. I find that this practice is essential for sustainable wellbeing. You don't have to do anything extravagant like hiking or camping, though if that is part of your routine, then by all means do it. Being out in nature can also look like taking a walk, stepping outside on your front porch, gardening, or simply gazing out of your window, taking in the scene outside.

Healthy, Mindful Movement: Moving our bodies is a beautiful way to release stress, build up endorphins, and get out of our heads for a while. Ask your body what it would like more of or less of. For a while I thought I "should" do more high intensive interval training (HIIT), but when I asked my body what it wanted, I was floored when I discovered it was yoga and gentle walking. From then on, I've deferred to what my body wants rather than what Instagram tells me I ought to be doing. I encourage you to do the same.

If you are not able-bodied, have sustained an injury, or have medical reasons for limiting movement, you can still engage in breath work, adaptive yoga, dance classes for all, or anything that allows you to move creatively within your body's capacity. There are some incredible teachers out there who specialize in these practices aimed at relieving stress and improving cardiovascular function. There are even free classes on YouTube that support fitness for all levels and body types. If you have the means, I encourage you to work with a practitioner who can support your physical needs in an honorable and safe way.

Regular Meals: Eating regular meals is way of engaging in self-care. Find foods that align with your value system and let them nourish and sustain you. Feeding ourselves regularly is an important part of tending to our bodies with care. If this has been a struggle for you, start small. Make a commitment to focus on treating at least one meal a day as a gift you are giving to your body. You might even consider mentally giving thanks to the incredible people and energy that has gone into growing and delivering your food. Sometimes taking a moment to appreciate this journey can add a layer of mindfulness and gratitude to the simple act of taking in nourishment.

Boundaries: We'll definitely get into this in the chapter on boundaries, but for now I'd like for you to consider where you can build in more boundaries for yourself around your time, emotions, and physical space. What would you like to start saying "yes" to in your life? Honoring (and knowing) our boundaries is a lifelong skill that requires consistent effort, awareness, and courage to put into practice. Go easy on yourself if this is an area you struggle with. Hopefully, with building community, working with a therapist, reading this book (and others), you will begin to discover new and creative ways to set boundaries without anxiety or guilt.

All Emotions Have Importance

As you read this book and work on your healing, you may find yourself experiencing a range of emotions. That's a good thing! We are wired to feel a spectrum of emotions, and all of them are natural. There is no such thing as an emotion that is "wrong." All emotions are important. There will be moments when you will notice yourself feeling a great deal of resistance toward making changes in your life and challenging those unhelpful beliefs you took in. Don't fret. It's absolutely normal to resist what is unfamiliar. You don't have to get any of this "right," as that's truly not the goal. Nor does your healing need to look like anyone else's.

As you extricate yourself from the chains of narcissism, there may be instances where you find yourself tempted to put them back on, as that is what you know. You don't yet know the real freedom that awaits you as a result of having a solid relationship to yourself. When you reach that place of emotional liberation and start to see yourself accurately, you may feel as though the fog has lifted, allowing you to see what's truly possible for yourself. You'll know you've made strides when you no longer find yourself worrying about what your mother will think, stuck in that endless cycle of running on a hamster wheel that goes nowhere. Forming a relationship to ourselves feels like sweet self-companionship; the most real commitment one can make. As the saying goes, "the way out is through," and I believe you have exactly what it takes to get there. You are never alone when you are self-accompanied.

Chapter 2

DEFINING NARCISSISM

Maternal narcissism is one of the most painful and enduring wounds for daughters to experience. The women I work with, all in various stages of narcissistic abuse recovery, know the profound agony of being motherless, despite many of their mothers still being alive and well. Maternal narcissism takes motherhood and flips it on its head, perverting it into a performance where image is everything, and the only person that matters is mom. The adult daughters I've worked with have described their experiences as feeling like they were put into a performance they didn't ask to be in. Nothing felt real or authentic.

Maternal narcissism is an insidious force that often lies hidden in plain sight. Under the guise of motherhood, most outsiders will not see it, leaving daughters wondering if they've been making up their mothers' behaviors or simply being "bad daughters" to their perfectly "normal" mothers. What daughters don't realize is that they're perfectly sane in their assessments of their mothers; it's the outside world that is unfortunately blind to this narcissism. This blindness also extends to the narcissist herself. Your mother does not see reality accurately, nor does she see the impact that her actions have on you. The sad reality is that even if you could prove to your mother how she has hurt you, she still would not see it. Her fragile self-esteem could not afford the blow.

For most adult daughters, their mothers' narcissism lurks like shadows, trailing behind their backs where they cannot see. One researcher describes maternal narcissism as "a self-centered, self-reflecting pathology where a mother is incapable of placing her child's needs above her own."[5] She is essentially *blind* to her child's needs, thereby making her blind to her own narcissism.

Narcissistic personality disorder can be defined in several ways, but in short it is a pervasive and chronic disturbance in personality that is persistent throughout the lifespan. Many of you who are reading this are likely already acquainted with the definition of narcissism found in the *Diagnostic and Statistical Manual of Mental Disorders (DSM)*, which I would argue is incomplete and does not define narcissism in all of its layered presentations. For posterity, however, the definition will be included as a foundation to work from. According to the 5th edition of the *Diagnostic and Statistical Manual*, narcissistic personality disorder (NPD) is defined as "a pervasive pattern of grandiosity (in fantasy or behavior), need for admiration, and lack of empathy, beginning by early adulthood and present in a variety of contexts."[6] The *DSM* goes on to describe this disorder stating, "typical features of narcissistic personality disorder are variable and vulnerable self-esteem, with attempts at regulation through attention and approval seeking, and either overt or covert grandiosity. Characteristic difficulties are apparent in identity, self-direction, empathy, and/or intimacy."[7]

Elsa Ronningstam, a clinical psychologist who specializes in narcissism, provides another definition similar to that of the *DSM*: "patterns of fluctuating and vulnerable self-esteem ranging from grandiosity (in fantasy or behavior) and assertiveness to inferiority or insecurity, with exceptionally high standards, self-enhancing and self-serving interpersonal behavior, intense reactions to perceived threats, and compromised empathic ability."[8]

Underlying such an individual's presentation of grandiosity, lack of empathy, and a need to be considered above others is a fractured sense of self so deeply rooted that it no longer registers consciously. In *Narcissism: Denial of the True Self*, psychoanalyst Alexander Lowen, MD, has suggested that individuals with NPD need to rely on an *image* of themselves to compensate for a significant sense of fragility and shame. He states, "The narcissistic image develops in part as a compensation for an unacceptable self-image and in part as a defense against intolerable feelings. These two functions of the image are fused, for the unacceptable self-image is associated with the intolerable feeling."[9] He goes on to describe that as children, these future narcissists experienced repeated blows against their self-esteem, rendering them powerless against an all-powerful *other*.

---

5. Ingrid Butterfield, "The Myth of Jocasta and Maternal Narcissism," *Australian Psychiatry* 20, no. 2 (2012): 153–56. https://doi.org/10.1177/1039856212438952.

6. American Psychiatric Association (APA), *Diagnostic and Statistical Manual of Mental Disorders, 5th Edition* (Washington, D.C.: American Psychiatric Association, 2013), 669 (Kindle edition).

7. APA, *DSM 5*, 767 (Kindle edition).

8. Elsa Ronningstam, "Narcissistic Personality Disorder: A Clinical Perspective." *The Journal of Psychiatric Practice* 17, no. 2 (March 2011): 89–99.

9. Alexander Lowen, *Narcissism: Denial of the True Self* (New York: Simon & Schuster, 1985), 66.

With repeated injuries against their self-esteem, their only recourse has been to build and sustain a false self, one that is powerful, impervious to being vulnerable, and admired (loved) by all. When a narcissist experiences a feeling that threatens their self-image, they rely on defense mechanisms to shield themselves from the threat. This is where you come into play. Mothers who cannot experience their own vulnerability, real feelings, or needs will experience yours as an intrusion upon their lives. Since your mother likely did not receive any attunement for her emotions and needs as a child, she will feel resentful of yours. Maternal narcissists are developmentally young girls themselves. They are still looking for their mothers to finally see and appreciate them, but tragically this will never come. Instead, they look to you in hopes that you will fulfill their needs, which cannot be done either.

Underneath your mother's narcissism lies a profoundly insecure, shame-prone, and devalued sense of self that drives her need to feel special. It's hard to fathom that narcissists feel anything but superiority and a high degree of self-esteem. The façade of superiority is merely a balm against facing the deep inner chasm of emptiness that threatens to swallow them up at any time. The *Psychodynamic Diagnostic Manual*'s definition of narcissism (not too dissimilar from the clinical *DSM*) states this notion succinctly: "The characteristic subjective experience of narcissistic individuals is a sense of inner emptiness and meaninglessness that requires recurrent infusions of external confirmation of their importance and value."[10]

Narcissists who display overt symptoms of narcissism such as grandiosity, inflated superiority, and lack of empathy would never admit to their inner sense of emptiness. This would betray their image of invulnerability. The overt narcissist's personality traits act like a shield against acknowledging the deeper feelings of deficiency and inadequacy that lurk underneath. To recognize these feelings would be staring into an abyss, which can be highly disorienting. Narcissists with more depressive tendencies might be aware of their inner sense of emptiness; however, they would use it like a tool to induce guilt and caretaking from others in their lives. We'll discuss the differences between grandiose (overt) and depressive/vulnerable (covert) narcissism later on in this chapter.

The Narcissist as a Parasite

Narcissism itself can be thought of like a parasite in the way it operates within relationships. Julie Hall, in her book *The Narcissist in Your Life: Recognizing the Patterns and Learning to Break Free*, compares narcissism to parasitism, stating, "Individuals with NPD are always

---

10. PDM Task Force. *Psychodynamic Diagnostic Manual* (Silver Spring: Alliance of Psychoanalytic Organizations, 2006), 44–46.

seeking the attention and affirmation they did not receive at crucial developmental stages. Their incomplete sense of being compels them to seek self-worth externally. Narcissists as a human parasite take a heavy emotional and physiological toll on their 'hosts.'"[11]

Since narcissists need others to define themselves, they become parasitic, always looking for the next person to sustain their sense of self from. Of course, when individuals learn this and begin setting boundaries, the narcissist may retaliate. Some covert narcissists may resort to depressive spells, unconsciously attempting to induce guilt in the other, a subtle form of manipulation. In the natural world, a parasite leeches off of the host until eventually the host is killed and the parasite moves on to the next one. In psychological terms, the host doesn't die; however, more often than not, the host comes to feel depleted of her essence, and is likely to experience significant mental and physical health problems.

You may have symptoms or experiences such as these:

- Moderate to severe depression
- Chronic anxiety
- People-pleasing, self-doubt, and chronic self-blame
- Gastrointestinal distress like irritable bowel syndrome (IBS), Crohn's Disease
- Autoimmune conditions
- Sleep disorders
- Eating disorders
- Difficulty saying no
- Fear of others manifested as social anxiety
- Hypervigilance
- Fear of emotions—yours and others'
- Weak boundaries
- Dissociation

The parasitic bond forged between narcissistic mothers and their daughters leaves daughters in a chronic state of internal conflict. On the one hand, daughters are expected to deny their feelings and needs so as not to threaten their mothers. Yet, despite this, their mothers remain perpetually disappointed in them. This leaves daughters feeling as if they are never going to be good enough for their mothers. The truth, however, is that they won't be, because narcissists have expectations that are rooted in fantasy. You will never be good enough for

---

11. Hall, *The Narcissist in Your Life*, 129.

your mother, not because you are lacking or deficient, but because *no one* will ever be good enough for a narcissist.

Narcissists use the defense of projection as a means of denying their unwanted feelings. In many cases, their children become the bearers of these painful emotions, which eventually take a toxic form within the child.[12] *Projection* is a defense mechanism whereby an individual takes something within themselves that they don't want to have and "projects" it (like a film projector) onto others. If I don't want to feel guilt for not showing up to a birthday party on time, I might project that guilt onto the host, claiming that *they* are hosting this event at an absurd time. That *they* should be the one to feel guilty for starting so early, not me for running late. Narcissistic mothers do this repeatedly.

Children must learn to adapt to their environment to survive. When an environment is scary and toxic, children have to rely on their own defense mechanisms to make it through. For the most part, children believe what their parents tell them. When a narcissistic mother projects her sense of "badness," guilt, shame, or unworthiness onto her child, the child will internalize this as a "truth" about her. The greatest gift I hope to bestow to you is the recognition that you have internalized *false data*. You took on a belief that wasn't yours to take in the first place.

Your mother appointed you as the holder of her unwanted feelings and insecurities. She could not respond to your rich emotional life or needs without coming into direct contact with all the ways she was not attended to by her mother. Your authenticity threatened to reveal her inauthenticity. When an individual has a relationship to themselves, by standing firmly in who they are, they cannot be manipulated, swindled, or defined by a narcissist. For a narcissist, this leaves them with two options: Either the narcissist moves on by rejecting or dismissing the individual, or they become hostile, exploding with rage or imploding into victimhood. In the latter two reactions, the narcissist is attempting to guilt trip the person into compliance.

---

12. Daniel Shaw, *Traumatic Narcissism: Relational Systems of Subjugation* (New York: Routledge, 2013), 4.

BREAK FREE FROM NARCISSISTIC MOTHERS

◗ REFLECTION

What rejected aspect of herself did your mother project onto you?

....

....

....

....

....

How has this shown up in your life?

....

....

....

....

....

Can you identify when your mother projects her own guilt or shame onto you?

When she belittles you, what aspect of herself is she really belittling?

Narcissists deny reality, which means they are also denying parts of themselves. This denial of reality comes from early childhood experiences in which being their authentic selves was routinely rejected and scorned. As you are now aware, narcissists learned early on to disown their real selves in favor of a false self-image as a way to eradicate the pain or possibility of rejection. The problem with this is that the real self doesn't actually go anywhere. It's still there; it's just out of awareness. To keep it out of awareness, a narcissist must rely on their defense mechanisms, which perpetuate their denial of reality. This is why telling a narcissist that they have hurt you or made a negative impact on you tends to go nowhere. They truly cannot fathom that they have done anything wrong, so they continue on as if *you* are the problem.

What was the image your mother portrayed to the world? How did she go about maintaining this?

Let's take a moment to identify some of the ways you can return your mothers' projections back to her. Identify at least three things that were projected onto you. They can be things like "You're too needy," "It's weak of you to cry," and "You'll never amount to anything." Any judgment that was unfairly placed onto you can be regarded as a projection. Consider how those don't belong to you, and treat them like items you are returning to a store you no longer wish to shop at.

Some examples:

- "I was never the one who was weak. You were incapable of facing your own limitations."

- "I was not the all-bad child you made me out to be. No child deserves that label."

- "A failure? I never failed; it was you who couldn't bear failure or imperfection."

- "My body was always good enough and should never have been the container for your own body-hatred."

- "I was never bad the way you told me I was. Your judgment spread like a poison that I never agreed to ingest."

- "You couldn't let yourself feel, but I paid the price. My feelings were never the problem."

Your mother will go to great lengths to preserve her image and has no compunction about lying either.[13] She may retell stories that never happened or make subtle changes to real events to maintain her own (false) self-image. Other lies that narcissistic mothers may tell will come in the form of gaslighting. If you are not familiar with the term, *gaslighting* is when someone purposefully denies what is happening in reality to confuse and lead the other individual to believe they are crazy. Many adult daughters end up with a sense of confusion about what to believe and learn to distrust their sense of reality, including what their feelings are telling them. For instance, one woman told me that as a child, she would often cry when her father didn't come home from work on time. She told her mother that she was crying because she missed him and wanted to see him at dinner time. Her mother turned her daughter's tears against her, telling her that children should not cry when they're sad because it teaches them to be "weak." As an adult woman. she now struggles with showing anyone her natural feelings out of a fear that they will tell her the same thing. She has learned to relate to others as though they, too, would judge and ridicule her.

A narcissistic mother who belittles her child behind closed doors will present a loving and generous façade to the outside world. Because she is a master of denial, she will perceive her

---

13. Lowen, *Narcissism*, 54.

actions as necessary, and her daughter as the one being abusive *to her*. This kind of denial of reality is pathological, meaning it completely distorts and deletes the truth in favor of something that *doesn't exist*.

Attachment Science and Developmental Psychology

A child has a very limited sense of objective reality. Her subjective experience gets conflated with objective truth. If a child feels fear, her worldview becomes imbued with fear. When an adult feels fear, they have a better capacity of knowing that the fear does not define the entire world; fear is a state that will pass. When a child witnesses her mother fly into a narcissistic rage, she will relate to that rage as though she caused it. Because she has not yet differentiated herself from her mother, her mother's feelings will seem like her responsibility. Children experience their worlds through a very simple lens, primarily because their brains are not yet fully developed and it helps them navigate the terrain around them. Since children are highly vulnerable, they have to be able to make sense of their world in simple black and white terms. Ambiguity is too threatening. Babies are wired to connect to their mothers from day one and rely on them for everything ranging from their physical safety to their emotional regulation. No one has to teach babies to seek out their mothers; it's wired from within. This is a problem for babies with narcissistic mothers, but of course they don't yet know this.

When a child's hardwired needs get thwarted for some reason, she has to make sense of this. From infancy to adolescence, unmet needs can lead to significant psychological damage, creating a collapsed sense of self. Children make sense of the experience of having their needs go unmet by concluding that they are bad in some way. To put it another way, children expect their mothers to love them no matter what: it is a fixed part of human nature. When children do not receive this love, they can only come to one conclusion: It's me. They do not have the capacity to consider that their mother may be narcissistic (nor would they even be able to fathom this).

If you've been living with the belief that says, "if only I were a better daughter, I would have gotten the love I deserved," know that this is coming from the perspective of a child who needed to preserve the image of the "all good" mother. Children need to mentally keep their mothers intact in order to survive and will go to great lengths to preserve this relationship, often sacrificing themselves to "keep mother happy."

The unconscious belief is: "If mom is cruel to me, ignoring my cries, criticizing my painting, telling me how stupid I am for asking that question, then that must mean I'm wrong or bad." Children will develop these beliefs about themselves so that they can *do something about the situation,* which offers them a sense of hope. Accepting that their mothers are unavailable because of something outside of their control would invite chaos and fear into their lives and threaten their sense of safety. The need to feel safe and in a controlled environment is a natural need for all children. When the environment becomes unsafe, out of control, or dangerous, children contextualize it somehow and often assign themselves as the cause of the overwhelm (all unconsciously).

Narcissism and Its Impact on Psychological Development

Daniel Shaw, a significant voice in the literature of pathological narcissism, states, "Narcissistic parents demand their child's love in a way that already contains within it resentment and rejection of the child—because the narcissist can only give love conditionally."[14] He then states, "These children and later adults have become oriented to the known and/or imagined perceptions of others, not to a trusted internal voice of their own."[15]

This level of pathology from a mother is severely damaging to a child who is just discovering her own mind and body and who looks to her mother for security. When that security is conditional or lacking altogether, a child learns to hide perceived "bad" parts of herself from her mother to preserve the relationship and avoid rejection. These children eventually grow into adults who believe that others do not have the capacity to understand or accept them as they are. Daughters of narcissistic mothers have been oriented to believe that only certain parts of themselves will be accepted and use up vital energy pushing away or ignoring the parts that they believe will be unaccepted by the other.

Reclaiming who we are starts from rescuing the parts of ourselves we thought were "bad" or unacceptable. These parts have been unfairly judged and blamed for a crime they did not commit. Remember, you took in a lot of false narratives about your worth as a human being that will take time to unlearn. As you reclaim who you are and learn to separate from the false narratives you took in, you may notice a combination of relief and fear. That's normal. It may even be challenging for you to believe that these narratives are false. Consider the source from which they came from. Developmentally, your mother is very young and her

---

14. Shaw, *Traumatic Narcissism*, 7.
15. Shaw, *Traumatic Narcissism*, 7.

worldview is still in black or white. It's as if she cannot see color. Her perspective is going to be highly skewed. This begs the question: would you advise anyone else to believe your mother's narratives about them? Why or why not?

◪ EXERCISE: MANTRA

Consider a memory or recent experience in which your mother shamed or ridiculed you. Write out what happened and how you felt.

After you write down how you felt, I'd like you to practice saying one of these mantras instead.

- "I will not feel guilty for who I am or what I need."
- "This is your shame, not mine."
- "Your devaluation of me is a reflection of your own unmet needs."
- "You are responsible for the guilt you feel, not me."
- "I will not be shamed for what I feel."
- "Your words against me reflect how you feel about yourself."
- "This relationship was never about us; it was about you."
- "I will not be bullied into feeling bad about my boundaries (or needs, feelings)."
- "This is false data and doesn't reflect the truth about me."
- "I am whole, complete, and human. I am not the fixed state you believe I am."
- "I will not hold your guilt or shame. Those are your feelings to bear, not mine."
- "My own healthy guilt will tell me when I've wronged someone. Having boundaries and needs and holding myself with care is not a crime and does not deserve guilt."

Narcissism Continued

Let's go back to the definition of narcissism again and discuss the two subtypes: grandiose (overt) narcissism and depressive/vulnerable (covert) narcissism. The grandiose presentation is the more notorious one, as it is louder and more obvious. We see it reflected in social media, politics, and entertainment. This type of narcissism aligns most consistently with the *DSM's* definition: an inflated ego, no signs of empathy, talking over others, denying facts, appearing entitled and oblivious to consequences, and living in a fantasy of power.

In a paper on pathological narcissism and narcissistic personality disorder, researchers Aaron Pincus and Mark Lukowitsky define narcissistic grandiosity as "expressed behaviorally through interpersonally exploitative acts, lack of empathy, intense envy, aggression, and exhibitionism."[16] The inverse of this would be covert narcissism, which they define as "enacted by providing instrumental and emotional support to others but concurrently harboring contempt for the person being helped and secretly experiencing the situation as reflecting one's own specialness, goodness, or superior capabilities."[17]

Grandiose narcissists are so inflated by their own sense of superiority and entitlement, that they are essentially blinded to the way their behavior affects others. Narcissists of this subtype are largely preoccupied with their own sense of importance, externalizing any and all of their flaws or relationship problems onto others.[18] Underlying their grandiosity is an almost equally fragile self-esteem. According to the authors, "the grandiose narcissistic individual is more likely to regulate self-esteem through overt self-enhancement, denial of weaknesses, intimidating demands of entitlement, consistent anger in unmet expectations, and devaluation of people that threaten self-esteem. They have diminished awareness of the dissonance between their expectations and reality, along with the impact this has on relationships."[19]

Overt narcissists generally perceive themselves positively and believe their relationships are unaffected by their behaviors. These types of narcissists may be more inclined to challenge you outright if you share that they have negatively affected you. They might tell you that you are thin-skinned, whiny, or making a big deal out of nothing and need to "get over it." An overt narcissist is convinced that their version of reality is the only one that matters. To them, your version of events will only sound like a smear campaign against their perfectly

---

16. Aaron L. Pincus and Lukowitsky, Mark R. "Pathological Narcissism and Narcissistic Personality Disorder." *Annual Review of Clinical Psychology* 6 (2010): 426-427, https://doi.org/10.1146/annurev.clinpsy.121208.13121.5.

17. Pincus and Lukowitsky, 427.

18. Kelly A. Dickinson and Pincus, Aaron L., "Interpersonal Analysis of Grandiose and Vulnerable Narcissism," *Journal of Personality Disorders* 17, no. 3 (2003): 188-207, https://doi.org/10.1521/pedi.17.3.188.22146.

19. Dickinson and Pincus, 189.

reasonable behaviors. A grandiose narcissist will often resort to gaslighting, which, if you remember from earlier, is a phenomenon in which an individual claims that what you see, hear, or feel isn't really happening. Hence your perception of reality essentially starts to feel more like a dream, and the truth of it fades with every attempt to remember it.

More often than not, the clients I see would describe their mothers as fitting the second subtype: vulnerable (or covert) narcissism. Researchers Dickinson and Pincus describe covert/vulnerable narcissism as "overtly self-inhibited and modest, but harboring underlying grandiose expectations for oneself and others."[20]

Another indication of covert narcissism is an overidentification with being the martyr or victim. These narcissists perceive themselves as having "more problems than others," but also present as self-sacrificing.[21] In some cases, covert narcissists may become depressed and vaguely suicidal when their children or spouses attempt to set boundaries.

Marla

Marla, a woman in her mid-20s, shared with me how her mother would always fall into a depression whenever Marla would stand her ground. "My mom would become so distraught when I tried to set a boundary. It didn't even have to be all that severe. Once, she asked if I could come over to help her redecorate, and when I let out the tiniest sigh of exasperation, she took that and said, 'Well I guess my life just doesn't matter to you. You probably wouldn't care if I was dead, so I guess I'll just hang up now.'"

Her mother's sudden collapse was the inverted version of a grandiose narcissist's "I'm so great" routine. It's more common for a covert narcissist to use guilt as a tactic, as it gets the other to drop their boundaries and feel responsible for the narcissist.

Marla told me that when she was a child, her mother would use a slightly different tactic from collapsing into herself. She would use Marla as a prop to furnish her stage play of being "the perfect, self-sacrificing mother." When Marla was 15, she asked her mother if she could buy her a pair of new 7 for All Mankind jeans, the ultra-popular brand that teens and adults lusted over. Excitedly, Marla told her mother that everyone was wearing them and she wanted to get a pair too. Her mother, however, heard her request as something else: an accusation of her mother's ineptitude. Marla's mother came back saying, "I do so much for you. Do you know how much I sacrifice

20. Dickinson and Pincus, 188–207.

21. Kenneth N. Levy, "Subtypes, Dimensions, Levels, and Mental States in Narcissism and Narcissistic Personality Disorder," *Journal of Clinical Psychology* 68, no. 8 (2012): 886–897, https://doi.org/ 10.1002/jclp.21893.

in order to buy you clothes? I can't believe you would ask this of me and not even consider how I would feel about it."

Stunned, Marla learned from that day on that she should not ask her mother for anything. Her mother's parading around of her sacrifices came from a need to be admired and heroic. A hero, in a narcissist's world, is someone who is self-sacrificing. They carry a heavy burden for others, martyring themselves along the way. Ironically, those they "sacrifice" for may end up feeling worse as a result.

Adding to the definition of vulnerable narcissism, researchers Dickinson and Pincus state, "vulnerable narcissistic characters need others to respond favorably to them and to admire them regardless of their behaviors, beliefs, skills, or social status, but fear that others will fail to provide them with narcissistic supplies.... The vulnerable narcissist's fear is that he or she will not be admired. Furthermore, vulnerable narcissistic individuals experience significant injury and anger in response to perceived slights."[22]

Essentially, covert narcissists cannot tolerate being disappointed by others who do not meet their unrealistic expectations.[23] They expect others to share their perception of reality (i.e., their fantasy), and when this doesn't happen, when others do not comply with their fantasy, they become very antagonistic, shocked, and outraged.

You may recognize instances in your life when your mother has reacted disproportionately to the situation at hand, confusing you further. Ever so subtle, this type of narcissism whispers a contract to the other: "In order to have a relationship with me, you must agree with me at all times, never see me unfavorably, and always hold me in high esteem. It would also be preferable if you merge with me so that I don't have to relate to someone who might see things differently from me. In fact, to make sure this doesn't happen, I will imbue your every choice, thought, and feeling with shame and guilt so that you do not become someone outside of me."

You don't have to be a psychologist or diagnostician to recognize the signs of narcissism within your mother. Your emotions will tell you when her behavior is wrong, hurtful, or unfair/unjust. This is where daughters struggle the most. Their feelings were chronically mishandled and labeled as "weak," "dramatic," "silly," "untrue," or "bad," creating a long-standing internal conflict between what they know (i.e., what their feelings are telling them) and what their mothers are insisting is true.

---

22. Dickinson and Pincus, 203.
23. Dickinson and Pincus, 188–207.

Unlearning the Narcissist's Fantasy by Coming Back to the Body

A major pathway back to having an intact sense of self is to begin to trust your perceptions, feelings, and intuition. When you're able to hear the voice of your body and emotions, you'll discover a tremendous wealth of information from which to draw upon. The information of the body speaks in physical sensations, emotions, and impulses. When you learn the language of the body, you have a forever ally to help you assess how your relationships are doing, whether or not you feel seen and heard, whether you like or don't like something, and what you need moment to moment. The body is where we house our emotions, and soon you will discover their deeply integral role in your life.

We'll explore your emotions in another chapter, but right now I'd like to pause and have you check in with your body. Don't do this while you're driving or preoccupied, but instead practice it when you are at home or in a safe space.

◖ EXERCISE: BODY CHECK-IN

Take a moment to simply sit. Let your breath be smooth and steady. Rest your eyes on something in front of you or close them. Scan your body from head to toe, slowly going over each section of your body.

- Notice and describe any sensation that is coming to your awareness.
- What are you feeling now? Where in your body are you feeling it?
- If this sensation could speak, what would it say? What feelings might it be conveying?
- Are you aware of an emotion occurring now? What is it?
- Is your body sending you any signals of distress, tension, or discomfort? What are they? Notice where in your body they're located.
- Do you notice any impulses arising from your emotions? Simply observe them without judgment.

The more you can tune into what your body is telling you, the more integrated you become. We have a tendency in our culture to rely solely on our rational thinking and forget that the signals from our bodies play an important role in defining who we are and what we want.

How Narcissism Affects a Sense of Self

The reason that most, if not all, adult daughters of narcissistic mothers struggle with feelings of unworthiness, self-doubt, fear of rejection, and social anxiety, to name a few, comes back to how they internalized their mothers' treatment of them. If your every attempt at self-expression and building a healthy sense of confidence was put into question, criticized, or outright ignored, then the foundation from which you are constructing your identity will be fractured. Bella could never believe in her own worth or trust her natural intelligence because she was repeatedly told that her drive to go to grad school would end in failure. Her mother would comment, "Why on earth are you wanting to go to grad school? Don't you realize how competitive it will be? I don't think it's worth it for you." Amber internalized her mother's criticisms of her desires and learned to distrust this part of herself, leading her down a path of significant self-doubt and impostor syndrome.

Narcissistic mothers unconsciously place a veil of uncertainty over their daughters' minds by questioning and criticizing their daughters' decisions. Over time, daughters learn to automatically distrust their own desires and longings, taking with them an inner critic that puts them into a mental straitjacket. Since narcissistic mothers cannot bear to allow their daughters to have too much knowledge, capacity, or creativity, they will unwittingly tip the scales back in their own favor by making sure their daughters remain ambivalent. Like Princess Aurora pricking her finger on the spindle, narcissistic mothers put their daughters' dreams and ambitions to sleep.

Amber

Amber, a creative and aspiring woman in her 40s, spent most of her 20s and 30s chronically stuck in a state of perpetual doubt over her linguistic abilities. Amber had been in love with the idea of going to France and working at an embassy. Amber's mother was deeply threatened by her daughter's ambition, always finding ways to remind Amber that her language capacities paled in comparison to her own and would likely remain mediocre at best. Her mother made sure to plant the seed of doubt and uncertainty in Amber's mind, which kept her from following her dream of going to France, instead settling in a corporate job she hated.

Narcissistic mothers operate with an impoverished sense of self, always needing others to validate them, which makes raising a child nearly impossible, since children require their mothers to attend to their needs first and foremost. Raising a child is a deeply threatening experience for narcissistic mothers. Unable to self-regulate, these mothers use their children as extensions of themselves and place demands on them that the children cannot meet.

Many new parents who are not narcissists will struggle from time to time to provide their children with adequate attention and attunement. This is simply a fact of life. Parents will make plenty of mistakes with their children, but as long as they are willing to own them and make repairs, their children will learn that their parents aren't perfect and that's okay. These children will grow to accept their own flaws and limitations as normal too.

Ellen, whom we met in Chapter 1, believed that sharing her inner world with anyone would be met with hostility and judgment. Her narcissistic mother made it clear from the outset that "good girls" follow a particular script that is "acceptable" to the outside world. Ellen's natural proclivities of questioning the status quo were silenced and shrunk by her mother. Her mother was a covert narcissist, pretending to be a loving mother on the outside but internally seething about Ellen's uniqueness and rebellious nature. Ellen shared how her mother's narcissism was so subtle that she spent years believing that it was she who was being uncharitable toward her mother. Ellen's mother would remind her of how much she "sacrificed" for her, giving her a roof over her head and food to eat, which led Ellen to believe that perhaps she was being too demanding and a "bad daughter."

When Ellen courageously expressed her feelings to her mother, describing how her put-downs and criticisms of Ellen's personhood caused significant self-esteem issues, the response she got in return was, "What are you talking about? All I do is give you what you want, and yet when I share something that I feel, you call me a bad mother?"

You'll notice that Ellen never said "bad mother." This slip revealed her mother's own belief about herself. She constructed the "good mother" image out of necessity to keep her flaws as a mother out of awareness. Instead, she projected the "bad mother" narrative onto her daughter, so that she could accuse Ellen as being the one with that belief. And then Ellen could believe that she was the "all bad" daughter. You see how crazy-making these conversations can be. Over time, Ellen learned to keep her feelings to herself and simply go along with what her mother wanted so she didn't have to hear her criticisms. Eventually, Ellen started to do the same in other significant relationships as she got older. Fortunately, she recognized this habit of self-erasing and began a course of treatment where she learned how to strengthen her sense of self and to honor her identity with more freedom.

Take a moment now to name the ways in which your relationship with your mother has challenged your self-perception. What do you believe about yourself that you'd like to change? How do these beliefs hold you back in your life? If you were to change how you view yourself, what would you hope could change as a result? What would you do more or less of?

Narcissism and Attachment

Narcissism creates "relational trauma" or a "relational post-traumatic stress" for some adult children.[24] Trauma is not limited to war combat, car accidents, or witnessing violence. Relational trauma is something less visible to the eye. This type of trauma can be embedded within families who appear to be living the good life replete with the white picket fence. Of course, it is not only reserved for families that look fine. Relational trauma can be captured in many different family structures across all types of lifestyles, cultures, socioeconomic brackets, races, and nations. Narcissism does not discriminate.

Instances that may help define relational trauma include when a caregiver is doing the following:

- Demonstrating a lack of attunement to your needs
- Ignoring you when you are in distress
- Denying your right to personal space or physical integrity
- Placing you in a double bind (damned if you do, damned if you don't)
- Invalidating and invading your boundaries
- Giving you too much space, bordering on neglect, or not enough, bordering on enmeshment[25]
- Making you responsible for the emotional needs of your caregiver (essentially requiring you to become the parent, known as parentification)
- Chronically under-meeting your physical and emotional needs, feelings, and stages of development

To put this all into context, let's take Greta. Her mom was an enmeshed and covert type of narcissist prone to punishing Greta by withholding attention and using profound levels of guilt to manipulate Greta's behavior. On the surface, her mother didn't "look the part" of a classic narcissist. She was around during Greta's childhood, worked relatively consistently, and provided her with shelter, clothes, and food regularly. By all accounts, Greta also "looked the part" of a healthy and loved child. However, within their relationship was another story.

---

24. Shaw, *Traumatic Narcissism*, XV.
25. Anne Katherine, *Boundaries: Where You End And I Begin—How To Recognize And Set Healthy Boundaries*, (Boca Raton, FL: Parkside Publishing, 1991), 70.

When Greta was a teenager, she told her mother that she was struggling with what she thought was the beginning of an addiction. Instead of getting her the help she needed, her mother proclaimed that addiction was merely a phase that she would grow out of. Confused, and knowing that addictions were a serious matter, Greta felt that she could not challenge her mother, nor did she know how to seek services for herself. Deep down, her intuition told her that ignoring her addiction would cause more harm to her body and not be the healthiest way forward. It wasn't until a teacher became worried about Greta's declining grades that her mother finally remitted. But now she could use Greta's addiction to gain sympathy for herself, not Greta.

Brandy, another adult daughter of a narcissistic mother, told me a heartbreaking story about her ten-year-old self. One day after she came home from school, Brandy broke down into sobs, revealing that she had been bullied emotionally and physically by two other girls in her class.

Before we go on with the story, how do you imagine a healthy and concerned mother would respond? Hold that in your mind and hear it out.

Brandy's mom responded with irritation. "Why are you so needy, Brandy? Just tell those girls to fuck off. I really don't have time to hear this because today my boss told me that if I didn't get my paperwork in on time, I would be on probation. So I really can't hear your complaining."

How would you have responded to Brandy if she was your daughter? What would be the first thing you would do? How would you respond to her fear and sadness and help her through that experience?

I don't have to tell you why both Greta and Brandy's mothers' responses are deeply traumatizing; you already know the reason. These are just some examples of how relational trauma manifests. Children rely upon their mothers for emotional equilibrium and attunement. When their mothers repeatedly miss the mark, relational trauma ensues and their children adapt accordingly. In both cases, Brandy's and Greta's mothers had their own unresolved trauma they were not dealing with. Mothers who do not address their own trauma are likely to repeat it, traumatizing their children as a result.[26]

Consider the damaging messages Greta and Brandy may have internalized regarding their pain. I imagine it sounding like, "My body doesn't matter. If it hurts, I must conceal it. If it's being abused, I must ignore it. When others hurt me, I have to compare it to my mother's hurt."

---

26 Shaw, *Traumatic Narcissism*, 4.

To understand what makes narcissism traumatizing in the first place is to understand a little bit about developmental psychology and attachment theory.

When a child is born into this world, they need their caregivers in order to survive. A child without a caregiver will die quickly. Our survival instincts necessitate that we attach to our caregivers, regardless of how cruel or unavailable they are. Infant attachment is an innate, hardwired response to survive by maintaining a connection to caregivers. When our caregivers are nurturing, available, and responsive to our needs, we grow up learning that others are essentially trustworthy and that our needs and feelings will be responded to. This is called *secure attachment*, a term first coined by psychoanalyst John Bowlby.

Children's healthy emotional development gets stalled when their caregivers respond to them with indifference, aggression, or fear. As mentioned above, children are highly adaptable and will learn which emotions or needs are considered acceptable to their parents. These adaptations are ways in which the child has learned to regulate the parent. A child who expresses her valid anger toward her mother for not paying attention to her may come to learn that "mom gets anxious when I'm angry," and silence this part of herself. In future instances when her anger comes up, this will elicit an anxiety response. Soon, the child will come to experience anxiety in place of her anger. For a child, however, this is what she must do to preserve her relationship with her caregiver.

Because children need their parents and caregivers to be available for survival, they will do whatever it takes to maintain that connection.

Children mirror their parents in the way they behave or *don't* behave. Since children are highly pliant, they will adapt to their environments in whatever way they need as long as it keeps the relationship with their parents intact. If a child senses that her mother doesn't like it when she cries, she will unconsciously stifle her tears and attempt to rid herself of experiencing or noticing feelings like grief or sadness. The child will learn to associate her normal feeling of sadness, for instance, as a potential threat to her mother's wellbeing, which, in turn, threatens the wellbeing of the child. As the child learns to adapt in this way, she will naturally approach other relationships through this lens, which will affect her relationships in adulthood.

Growing up in the empty arms of a narcissistic mother means that you had to adapt yourself around her pathology, carefully monitoring what you said or didn't say, how you behaved, and what choices you made. Some of this was a conscious attempt at pleasing your mother or avoiding her ridicule, but most of it was unconscious, operating outside of your awareness. Fortunately, these unconscious patterns can be made conscious, where they can be reexamined in the light of day.

Attachment Styles

Let's talk about the various attachment styles and how they present.

John Bowlby and Mary Ainsworth are the founders of attachment theory, and many authors, scholars, and psychologists have added their findings to the research. Primarily there are four to five categories of attachment, which I will outline briefly. To go into detail about each category is beyond the scope of this book; however, links for further reading on attachment are provided in the bibliography. Dr. Phebe Cramer gives the reader a succinct overview of each category, which I have summarized here in my own words.

As we've discussed, secure attachment is when a parent or caregiver provides adequate responsiveness, warmth, and attunement to their child. They needn't be perfect parents, but good enough. These parents convey to their children that their feelings, needs, and individuality are important. A secure attachment gives a child a basic sense that *I am lovable and worthy; others are trustworthy and dependable.*[27]

Anxious, or insecure attachment, is characterized as being "uneasy and vigilant about threats to relationships; worried."[28] Anxious/insecure attachment has three different subtypes:

- **Preoccupied attachment**, where the sense of self and others could be conveyed as: "I am unworthy, bad and you are amazing, better than I am. I must stay in close proximity to you." This style could be described as clingy or codependent.[29]

- **Dismissive attachment**, which may resemble the early stages of narcissism, would have the person believe that "You are less than I am. I am great. I don't need you. You have no value to me." This type of attachment offers the promise of being better and superior, which has a self-protective strategy of keeping other people at a distance by labeling them as inferior. However, this does not necessarily mean that narcissism stems from this attachment style. Dr. Cramer states, "Because dismissive attachment involves a positive model of the self, narcissism may be unrelated to this attachment style."[30] Remember, narcissists have a negative image of themselves, not a positive one.

---

27. Phebe Cramer, "Narcissism and Attachment: The Importance of Early Parenting," *The Journal of Nervous and Mental Disease* 207, no. 2 (2019): 69-75, http://doi.org/10.1097/NMD.0000000000000919.

28. Peter Lovenheim, *The Attachment Effect: Exploring the Powerful Ways Our Earliest Bond Shapes Our Relationships and Lives* (New York: Tarcher Perigee, 2018), 17.

29. Cramer, 1.

30. Cramer, 1.

- Last is a **fearful attachment**, also known as disorganized attachment, according to Mary Main, who discovered this attachment style.[31] [32] This kind of attachment can usually be understood as being the result of a chaotic environment and parent-child relationship. In this category, the child seeks support and soothing from a caregiver who is both scary and scared,[33] making proximity overwhelming.

To make sense of this, children will often internalize their caregivers' chaos, believing it is due to something wrong with them. When caregivers are chaotic and frightening, a child is placed into a double bind. On the one hand, her caregiver frightens her and she wants to get away, but on the other hand she needs to rely on her caregiver to survive, so she must bypass her fear and endure. In some instances, this leads to dissociation. The primary theme of self and other would be something like: "I am bad and unworthy; you are hostile and scary. The only way to cope is to dissociate, shut down, or freeze."

Regardless of your attachment style, you are not doomed to live out this type of relating forever. Research has shown that repeated long-term involvement with a healthy and secure person, such as a therapist, can offer what is called *earned secure attachment*, which means that you can reprogram your attachment style to be secure.[34]

Earned secure attachment is not achieved in a few therapy sessions, but can be experienced through ongoing relational therapy that fosters a sense of safety and trust within the therapeutic relationship, and eventually cultivating trust within the self. Working through trauma with a therapist in a gradual, respectful, and intentional way can set the stage for something new to emerge. Often, clients come out of these experiences feeling more aligned with their authentic selves and trusting that what they feel *matters*.

How Did My Mom Become a Narcissist?

Many factors may have contributed to your mother's narcissism: having her own narcissistic or emotionally immature parents, environmental stressors, inadequate attunement from caregivers, physical and emotional abuse, bullying, nature and nurture. Primarily, however,

---

31. Kenneth N. Levy, Johnson, Benjamin N., Clouthier, Tracy L., Scala, Wesley J., and Temes, Christina M. "An Attachment Theoretical Framework for Personality Disorders," *Canadian Psychology/Psychologie Canadienne* 56, no. 2 (2015): 197-207, https://doi.org/10.1037/cap0000025.

32. Robbie Duschinsky, "The Emergence of the Disorganized/Disoriented (D) Attachment Classification, 1979-1982," *History of Psychology*, 18, no.1: 32-46, http://dx.doi.org/10.1037/a0038524.

33. Duschinsky, "Emergence of Disorganized/Disoriented Attachment Classification," 32-46.

34. Lovenheim, *The Attachment Effect*, xx.

the literature confirms that difficulties with attachment play a huge role in how narcissism develops, namely as it is "characterized by impoverished interpersonal relationships."[35]

Going back to Dr. Cramer's work on narcissism and attachment, she states that "narcissism is likely to be related to preoccupied and fearful attachment, both of which are based on a negative model of the self, against which narcissism is a defense."[36] This may help to answer part of the question surrounding why your mother became a narcissist. As you may remember, in both fearful and preoccupied attachments, a person views the other as both a threat and a source of survival. Narcissists operate from this viewpoint: You threaten your mother on some level, yet she needs you to sustain her self-image.

Many daughters find themselves stuck ruminating over the whys of their mother's narcissism, leading to further questions about their mothers in general. Here are some common statements and questions I have heard daughters make:

- I need to know why she is the way she is.
- Even though I understand her diagnosis logically, I still feel this need to know for sure if she is actually a narcissist.
- I wish there was a way I could prove that my mom is a narcissist. My sister/brother denies that she's a narcissist and thinks I'm just being too sensitive.
- I need to know what part of her is narcissistic and what part of her is not so I can know how to react to her.
- Is she all that bad? Maybe I'm making this up.
- Shouldn't a mother be loving toward her daughter? I don't understand the mechanics of how a mother could be so cold. (This is usually where daughters begin to wonder if they caused the problems in their relationship.)
- If she is a narcissist, why the hell did she decide to have children?
- Can narcissism be unlearned?
- What if I'm making a huge mistake about her? Maybe I'm being unreasonable.

Sadly, these questions will not give daughters the answers they crave. Underlying these questions is a longing for a mother who will never come. Intermingled within these questions lies the impotent frustration of never being able to "know for sure" about a mother's narcissism. Daughters grappling with the truth of their mother will experience a myriad of emotions ranging from bone-deep grief to diffuse rage. You may have found yourself

---

35. Levy et al., "An Attachment Theoretical Framework for Personality Disorders," 197–207.
36. Cramer, 1.

BREAK FREE FROM NARCISSISTIC MOTHERS

questioning if your mother really is narcissistic more often than not, feeling the familiar pang of doubt distort your memories and perceptions. I've had clients tell me that they wish narcissism was as tangible and obvious as cancer is, so that they could have some kind of certainty that would extinguish their doubts. Ultimately, this need to know for sure stems from an ingrained habit of *not believing your own point of view*. Your mother's narcissism has affected your ability to trust yourself, essentially training you to default into self-doubt.

While it makes sense for you to want proof of your mother's narcissism, you don't actually need it in order to move forward. In fact, most individuals with Narcissistic Personality Disorder will never present themselves for therapy, let alone an assessment, and many clinicians will not recognize the signs of covert narcissism either.[37] Your *feelings* will tell us all that we need. Your emotions, beliefs, and behaviors will offer us a wealth of insight. When you are needing to know for sure if your mother is a narcissist, despite the evidence from your own experiences, you are putting the authority in someone else. While this isn't wrong, as it's natural to want to understand that which we don't, consider what would happen if the answer was no? Would you feel better or worse? What would getting this proof grant you that you cannot give to yourself already?

◗◖ REFLECTION

Let's come back to your feelings and experiences in relation to your mother as a way to begin the identification of her narcissism. Here are a few questions to ask yourself. Write out the answers. Don't try to overthink it, just go with your first instinct. Let's focus on what happens to you when you are either in her presence, thinking about calling her, or planning to see her in the near future.

What immediately happens in your body when you are around your mother?

37.. Hall, *The Narcissist in Your Life*, 10-11.

When you are talking with your mother, what emotions do you feel?

What is the biggest "oh no" thought that comes into your mind when you see your mother (i.e., "Oh no, she's going to want to talk about that political debate from last night.")?

Do you feel listened to when you're with your mother?

Can you share your feelings with your mother? Why or why not?

....

....

....

....

....

....

Do you trust your mother?

....

....

....

....

....

....

What is the primary way you feel when around her?

....

....

....

....

....

....

In what ways do you feel you have to constrict yourself or behave differently when around her?

When you share an accomplishment, how does she respond?

Would your mom be on the list of people who make you feel good?

If you were to set a boundary with your mother, tell her you need space, or reveal that you are unavailable for something, how would she respond? How would her response make you feel?

Do you trust that if you told your mom how her actions hurt you she would make a repair with you in a meaningful way? If not, what would her response be?

What would your mom say about the fact that you're in therapy or attempting to better yourself in some way?

I don't need to have a "results" page for you to know that your mother is a narcissist. The answers you've provided above will be your knowing. Remember, a narcissist doesn't *always* reveal their narcissism in the most obvious ways. Narcissists can be charismatic and engaging, depending on the situation. You likely have interactions with your mom that feel loving. In those moments, you'll question if she really is all that bad and wonder if maybe you're overreacting. I can assure you that you are not. And let's be truthful here: she may not be that bad *all the time*. This is what makes being in a relationship with narcissists confusing. They aren't always unpleasant to be around.

In her book *The Narcissist in Your Life*, Julie Hall puts it another way. She states, "One of the most disorienting things about narcissists is that they can be nice."[38] Just when you are feeling confident in declaring your needs, boundaries, and feel ready to finally break free from narcissistic abuse, your narcissistic mother suddenly becomes accommodating, attentive, and seemingly capable of showing you she cares. When this happens, it can feel as if the rug not only was pulled out from under you, but also was never there in the first place.

This is often when a daughter begins to melt under the warm glow of her mother's shift in personality. Having the mother they always dreamed of feels intoxicating. Often the refrain, "am I just making this up?" glides over their mental framework like a slide on a projector. Narcissistic mothers will shift like this; not because they are truly wanting a connection with you, but because it offers them validation about their own "goodness" as a parent.[39] Probably the hardest truth to grasp is that even in these moments, they are still serving themselves. It truly is not about you, and this display of warmth or love toward you is not authentic. As a clinician, I feel the deepest empathy for my clients when their mothers change into this disguise, offering the illusion of hope that is so often shattered.

As you experience your mother's sudden change in mood and behavior, you will find yourself both confused and hopeful. While hope is a wonderful thing, I would advise you to tread lightly as you notice this feeling. When you're finally getting the loving attention you've craved, it's easy to forget all the ways in which you were treated before. If you aren't sure how to proceed, let's identify a few things you can do to stay intact.

1. Recognize that this behavior is fleeting.

2. Stay true to your boundaries despite the loving change.

3. Take in the good behavior the way you would appreciate a beautiful sunset: allow yourself to enjoy the scenery, and recognize it as a moment of beauty. We can appreciate a sunset for what it is and simultaneously acknowledge that the next sunset may not look like this one. In fact, the remaining 364 sunsets may be obscured by cloudy skies or blasted by rain. The point is not to get attached to the orange hues and pink undertones; they will change, but you can appreciate their temporary presence.

4. Lovingly respond to yourself with an acknowledgment of the situation.

5. Give plenty of care and support to the part of you that has needed her mother's love. Let this part of you know that her feelings and needs matter to you.

---

38. Hall, *The Narcissist in Your Life*, 220.
39. Hall, *The Narcissist in Your Life*, 220–221.

6. Remember the bigger picture: your mother will not remain like this.

7. Remind yourself that her change in behavior is not really about you.

When narcissistic mothers present in a contradictory manner, such as going from cold and withholding to suddenly being warm and apologetic, daughters get mixed messages, leaving them highly vulnerable. It is in these moments that daughters may default to doubting themselves, second-guessing their boundaries, and even feeling a measure of guilt for having them in the first place. Can you relate? Doubt has been a constant companion in your life. You had to *learn* to doubt yourself. Doubt, like anything else, has to be learned and reinforced in order for it to become a habit. Narcissists drill this into their daughters from day one.

This takes us to the next section: common themes experienced among adult daughters of narcissistic mothers.

Can you find yourself in any of these case examples?

- Experiencing significant guilt for setting boundaries with your mother
- Feeling anger toward your mother that gets turned on yourself and then finding yourself feeling depressed
- Feeling as though you, your siblings, and other caregivers are actors following a script
- Believing that you are overreacting when you begin talking to a therapist about the issues stemming from your childhood
- Feeling confused by why you feel so "bad" when your childhood looked fairly "normal"
- Sensing that your mom is either using you to benefit her needs or competing with you
- Noticing that if you don't play along with the family script, your mom doesn't know how to respond to you
- Experiencing shame for the way you feel and comparing yourself to other daughters
- Wishing you had a relationship to your mom the way your friends do with theirs
- Feeling as though you are parenting your mother rather than the other way around
- Experiencing anxiety about how your mom will talk to your spouse or partner (expecting her to be hypercritical)

Kathy

Kathy always felt that she had disappointed her mother in some form or another. As we worked together, she began to make room for her own feelings and was stunned to recognize that she felt significant anger toward her mother for all the ways she undervalued, belittled, and ignored Kathy most of her life. When Kathy began to get in touch with this righteous anger, she could only get so far, as something would stop her. I noticed Kathy deflate like a balloon, when moments before she was experiencing a powerful and energizing emotion.

A common phrase she would say to me was, "What's the point in feeling my anger? Why can't I just get over it already?" I felt great empathy for the part of her that wanted to move on and no longer be conflicted about her mother. During these moments, it was as if a great wall came between us, preventing both of us from giving our attention to the painful feelings hiding behind it. We can't get over our experiences if we don't allow ourselves to feel our emotions about what we experienced. As the saying goes, "the only way out is through."

There are two types of pain: productive pain and unproductive pain.[40] Productive pain is when we let ourselves feel into our painful emotions like grief, sadness, and anger. Emotions are forces inside of us that require our attention in order to lead to resolution and to potentially transform into something new. Unproductive pain would be an emotion that we vehemently try to avoid by pushing it down, turning away from it, which leads us toward avoidance and distraction.

If you have ever experienced grief, anger, or jealousy and tried to distract yourself from the pain by getting on your phone, not allowing yourself to cry, or numbing out, then you have experienced unproductive pain. When we have to find new avenues to get away from our feelings, then we unintentionally create more problems for ourselves, leading to worse experiences like anxiety or depression. Even though emotions can be painful, being with them is what actually leads to their resolution.

---

40. Bridget Quebodeaux, LMFT, in discussion with the author, 2021

Helen

Helen, a successful manager at a sought-after tech company, relied heavily on her intellect to get her through difficult moments. A self-made woman, she touted her ability to stay focused on the task at hand without becoming emotional or over-whelmed as being the reason for her success. The problem, however, was that this tactic did not work in her relationships. Not knowing what she felt and relying solely on her intellect to make decisions left her routinely unhappy. Helen told me, "I don't even know how to have an emotion without overthinking it." I would ask her, "How would your mom typically respond to you when you were sad or angry as a child?" Helen responded, "She would go completely rational and told me that whatever I was feeling was just a state of mind, so I should change my perspective. I took that to heart and found that anytime I felt a strong emotion, I would shut it down and try to rationalize it away. This also happens when my girlfriend is having a strong emotion. I don't know what to do, so I get really distant and shut down. I've just been like this for so long that I don't know an alternative."

Helen was caught up in a habit of intellectualizing and rationalizing away her feel-ings. It was as if her head were disconnected from her body, and this disconnection left her completely out of touch with what she felt. Helen learned from her mother to approach her emotions as forces that should be controlled, not explored with curios-ity. Without a connection to what we feel, we cannot truly know ourselves or what we want. Helen learned that when she disconnected from her feelings, she couldn't navigate the intricacies of her relationships, or even identify what she wanted, and this left her without a map.

Mary

Mary, a woman in her late 20s with a bubbly personality, told me she always felt that she had to take care of her mother's needs and be "what she wanted me to be." One day toward the end of our session, Mary confessed that she felt compelled to be what I needed her to be too. "I notice that whenever you ask me a question, I feel this sense like I'm going to disappoint you if I don't get it right. I know that sounds crazy because there isn't a right answer, but I still feel like I'm doing something wrong. Does that make sense?" Of course, logically Mary knew this wasn't true, but logic doesn't quell the underlying childhood fear that "Mommy is going to be disappointed in me." Mary knew that I was a safe person to express herself to, yet her implicit memories of never feeling like she could get it "right" dominated our interactions. It's not through logic that we experience change, but through our emotional experiences. Mary had to allow herself to have a new kind of relationship with me, one where she could relate to *me*, rather than the projected image of her mom that was placed onto me.

Will My Mom Ever Change?

This is not something I can answer with absolute certainty, as every case is so different. However, what I can say is that your mother's narcissism is not going anywhere. Personality disorders like narcissism and sociopathy are almost immune to treatment, as individuals with these disorders will a) likely never show for therapy in the first place, and b) be unwilling to change these entrenched characterological traits that are etched deeply in their personality.

The most painful truth is that it is incredibly unlikely that your mother will come around to see the error of her ways. Nor will she likely be more loving and attentive, or own up to her faults and the hurts she has caused you. For some, this realization can be a relief, since so many daughters spend much of their mental energy wishing, ruminating, and even changing themselves in order to get the mother they so long for. For others, this prediction is devastating, particularly for the little girl part of them that is still wishing and waiting for her mother to finally see and accept her. When the truth of your mother's personality disorder is accepted as a reality, then the focus needn't be on contorting yourself to get her to change. The focus can be on putting energy back into yourself to change *in relation to your mother*. The acceptance of this fact doesn't dissolve the pain of losing a hoped-for mother, but it does allow for something new to emerge within yourself.

Chapter 3

HOW WE BIRTH OUR OWN MOTHERS

Bring to mind the image or feeling that comes up when you say the word "Mother." Simply drop into your body and notice your physiological and emotional reactions. You may notice your body drinking in the word like nectar, giving you a sense of peace and nourishment. On the other end of the spectrum, you may feel a kind of disgust or disdain. You may also notice an absence of feeling that registers as hollow and empty, devoid of any life or energy. There is truly no wrong answer. Just notice and be present with what comes up.

Now what happens when you say "my mother"? Does your body respond differently? How about your emotions? If your emotions could speak, what would they say? Anger would tell us that there may be an association with her violating your boundaries and disregarding your needs. Fear would alert us to a sense that you are in danger, either physically or emotionally. Grief may tug at your heart, letting you know how much you've lost and long for. There may also be hope for a better relationship with your mother and a sense of being unwilling to let go.

Probably the most complicated relationship on the planet is the one we have with our mothers. From birth, we are wired to depend on her, to reach for her in times of distress and to eventually separate from her enough to live a life that is independent. Maternal narcissism takes what is already a complex relationship and wraps it in a hornet's nest before it gets dropped into an abyss. Daughters whose mothers are narcissists learn to live for their mothers, often out of a result of fear. By living for their mothers, I mean that these daughters learn what their mothers want out of them and attempt to contort themselves into the perfect package. As a result of conditioning, a deeply toxic inner mother develops for these daughters, just like a poison being administered slowly over time, the effects become normalized, which is when this inner mother becomes most dangerous.

This chapter is about how you can birth your own mother, one that responds to what you need and can be accessed at any time. This mother can be expansive, where she takes up a welcomed residency inside and is a gentle witness to all that you are. Her connection to you is deeply rooted; ancient as a redwood tree and fiercely protective. This mother knows you intimately and can be accessed at will for guidance and love. She is you, yet she is created by you. This is her origin story.

Bethany Webster, author and "mother wound" expert, offers insight into how we may forge a connection to the inner mother. In her book *Discovering the Inner Mother*, Webster states that "intergenerational healing requires that we learn how to embody the very things we never received, to be the loving presence that we longed for ourselves, the unconditional, benevolent presence that's there no matter what."[41]

The inner mother is a presence that *knows you*. Her capacity to give is unending, and when you are tapped into her, you feel held and nurtured. The first tool we must take with us on the quest to find our inner mother is curiosity. Any time we are doing something new, we must have access to curiosity so that we can take in new information and let go of outdated beliefs that no longer apply. Seeking out your own inner mother cannot be done fully without the willingness to be curious and open to being in unfamiliar territory. So often this work is akin to traveling through a dense forest using the wisdom of nature, rather than relying on a complete map. In many respects, you are learning to trust your own inner wisdom and truth. This is not an easy task, but it's one you're capable of taking on.

Curiosity is best defined as a willingness to perceive *without judgment*. The part of us we are defining as the inner mother is built on this foundation. When you are connected to your curiosity, you are inviting a different type of perspective to take shape. You are letting go of preconceived notions and replacing them with a beginner's mind that asks, "What would it be like to be without this belief?" The world we live in demands certainty, and rips curiosity right out of its cradle. One of the ways back to curiosity is by letting go of the need to be certain about what we think we know. If you can gently allow yourself to lean into uncertainty, you give yourself permission to relate to reality as it is unfolding in front of you, rather than reality as you think it is, which is largely based on assumptions.

41. Bethany Webster, *Discovering the Inner Mother: A Guide to Healing the Mother Wound and Claiming Your Personal Power* (New York: William Morrow and Company, 2021), xviii..

Self-curiosity, when it is directed at what is happening within us, can offer a space to pause. What is the story I'm telling myself? Where am I getting my information? Could this be better explained as an assumption rather than an objective truth? Am I feeling this way because a need is not being met? What would feel good for me in this moment?

All of these questions allow us a moment to reflect and get closer to ourselves in ways that our real mothers may not have been capable of doing. I once had a client tell me that the idea of being mothered was as foreign to her as quantum physics. "I don't even understand the mechanics of it. When you ask if I was mothered, I can tell you that yes, I had a mother, but I also had a pair of shoes...."

The you-mother also says "no" without second-guessing her right to that word. When an experience or person is not feeling supportive or good for you, or is causing some kind of harm, *no* is the only word that is needed. The inner mother may also lovingly support you by limiting any part of you that wants to disconnect, avoid, or zone out, and nudge you toward being present to the emotion that is activated in the moment. Her voice is without judgment when she encourages you to be with your feelings. In this space, she speaks from love rather than criticism. There will never be a "what's wrong with you?" question emanating from the you-mother. A question she is likely to ask is "Are you hurting? Do you need care? How can I best support you?"

Voice and *presence* are two facets of the inner mother that allow for healing. When you give voice to what you feel or need, you are acknowledging your right to speak truth. In order to speak from this place, it is necessary that we acknowledge it is our birthright to do so. Speaking from *voice* can take you into deeper places within your relationships and disrupt cycles of abuse by bringing it out of shadow. Your voice allows you to take responsibility for your needs and gives you the tools to cut through constrictive cords that have kept you silent. Voice needn't be limited to speaking words; it can be activated through writing, art, and embodied movement. We speak truths in many different forms and the more we do this, the stronger our voice becomes.

Presence, as the name suggests, is the practice of being present to what we feel or need without turning away. If you have a spiritual practice, you might think of presence as the feeling of being connected to a higher power. Presence is an active approach to witnessing ourselves without judgment. It is through presence that we notice and allow *all* feelings to arise and speak their truth. From this place, we are showing up for ourselves as we are, not as we think we need to be. Our needs can finally take up the space they so deserve and be given recognition for their importance to us.

Let Go of These Concepts

As you consider the idea of cultivating, birthing, and connecting to your inner mother, let's pause for a moment and reflect on what you may need to let go of in order to do this work.

CONCEPT 1—That there is an end goal: While an end goal can serve many purposes, like offering a sense of completion, this work is ongoing. It's a *direction* you are going in, rather than a destination. Letting go of the notion that you must arrive at some final place may actually free you to find the path that leads you to better *places*, while journeying again and again. As is true for any journey into new places, there will be moments of terror, fatigue, and boredom. However, without those challenges, the moments of beauty and awe for the landscape around you wouldn't be as meaningful.

CONCEPT 2—That you must be a perfect mother to yourself: Impossible. There is no perfect mother and the more we try to find her, the more disappointed we'll be when she doesn't show up. The idea behind self-mothering includes allowing for imperfections and blunders. No mother, whether she exists inside of us or outside, will be perfect or ideal. The mother that we are cultivating together is one that is present, curious, and capable of making mistakes. Just as we are learning to accept ourselves as flawed human beings, we must also do so for our inner mother.

CONCEPT 3—That you must be productive, always moving forward and never backwards. As enticing as that may sound to the part of us that has been trained to "better ourselves" and conquer our limitations, the opposite will be true for your healing. Resting, slowing down, taking breaks, and pausing for long periods of time are acts of rebellion against a dominant culture that tells you to "be more." Recognize that just *being* is enough. Disobey a little. Break out of confining norms that tell you what you "should" be. Honor your innate wisdom by listening to what your body and emotions are telling you.

Your Inner Mother Is for You, Not Your Mother

Your inner mother does not want you to sacrifice yourself any longer. She is sweetly telling you that you don't have to try to fit into a shape that doesn't belong to you. For much of your life, you've been taking responsibility for things that aren't yours, like your mother's feelings and her insecurities. The inner mother you are creating is here to mother *you*, not your mother. As painful as it may be to realize that no matter what you do, you cannot change your mother, what I hope you will find is the courage to accept yourself regardless. The best thing you can do for you and for your mother is to allow her to be responsible for herself. Her time is up, and that's a very good thing.

You can do this by:

- Recognizing your own triggers: What are the behaviors that your mother displays that cause you to feel that her emotions or behaviors are your responsibility?

- Staying connected to the truth: You cannot take on her feelings or be responsible for her emotions or behaviors. She must do those things on her own.

- Being a separate person: You do not have to merge yourself with your mother. Her hobbies, interests, and values do not have to be yours. What are the qualities and aspirations within yourself that set you apart from her?

- Listening to your emotions and honoring your boundaries: Your emotions will tell you when a boundary is being crossed. You'll notice yourself feeling anger, discomfort, and a sense of unease. Honor what your emotions are telling you. You are entitled to what you feel and what you need no matter what.

Unsurprisingly, cultivating a connection to your inner mother means that you must forge the same connection to your inner child. This little girl needed so much from her real mother, and what she didn't get is something you can offer to her now by listening to her feelings, responding to her needs, and offering her protection.

Being your own mother is also about honoring that which makes you sovereign. It's about no longer speaking from a place of complicity, but from a place of self-empowerment where the risk of being small and quiet outweighs the risk of being real. There is no greater sense of freedom than being able to speak truthfully. In *Discovering the Inner Mother*, Bethany Webster defines this as "disruptive truth-telling," which she describes as a practice in which we empower ourselves to have difficult conversations in service of our own healing.

Disruptive truth-telling is not only limited to verbally stating the truth, but also includes acting in new ways that support our evolution. Our intuition, body wisdom, and connection to self are all ways that disruptive truth-telling can show up and speak to us. The process must begin by looking inward so that we may learn to recognize the signals and cues emanating from within that tell us of our own truths. For example, I once found myself caught in a very familiar dynamic in which I placed myself last in favor of tending to another in my personal life. While normally I would check in with myself to make sure I had enough bandwidth to offer such tending, this time I bypassed that process entirely. What ended up happening was a building of resentment and frustration. I obliged this person out of an old habit learned from childhood where keeping the peace was more important than honoring my own needs. It's so important that if you find yourself caught in a familiar dynamic that you begin by acknowledging how deep this habit goes and give yourself compassion for stepping back into it. Like any unlearning of deeply held beliefs, it's important we give ourselves grace and acknowledgment of our efforts. You will undoubtedly find yourself caught back in an old cycle from time to time, as you are human. Remind yourself that this is normal, and know that you can offer yourself unlimited support as you practice your unlearning.

The inner work that you are doing will challenge long-held beliefs that aren't working for you anymore. They are effectively the beliefs of a child who had to use her limited, yet brilliant, survival mechanisms to cope with the world around her. The child you once were needed to keep her mother happy and her environment peaceful, so she sacrificed a lot in order to make this happen. Now, as an adult, those strategies keep you disconnected from your needs and create a lot of turmoil. If you could dissolve these old strategies, what would you replace them with to get your needs met this time? How would it feel to show up in your relationship with more freedom to express yourself and your needs authentically?

▶️ EXERCISE: LEARNING TO SEPARATE—WHAT I LEARNED AND HOW I FEEL

As an exercise, I'd like for you to fill in the circles on page 54. In the first circle, write out all the ways you were taught to behave, survive, feel, and think. This could include the following: be a pleaser at all costs; keep your needs to yourself; when mom is mad, that means no dinner; if mom is yelling at me, leave my body; if I feel sad, I have to cry alone in my room.

In the second circle, write out how you feel about these learned habits. How is it for you to look at the ways you had to keep yourself hidden out of view? After writing how you feel, take a moment to identify the costs these habits have on your life now. What is motivating you to change them? What are you hoping for as a result of changing them?

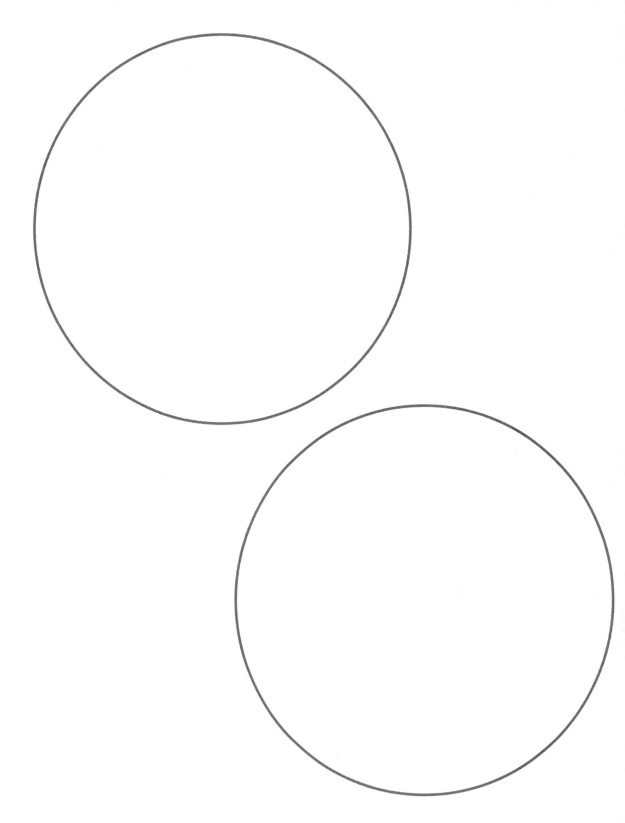

◪ EXERCISE: IDENTIFYING THE TRIGGERS

What are some of the external or internal triggers that catapult you back into those old survival mechanisms? An external trigger could look like a partner expressing their feelings to you and it activating the part of you that learned to take care of others at the expense of your own needs. Or it could be that your boss has something to tell you, and your first instinct is to cry, readying yourself for criticism. An internal trigger could look like you having a feeling that was not permitted as a child, which now causes you to become quite anxious. Perhaps you are at a party and someone has said something truly offensive. You might notice a flash of heat across your face and in your abdomen, which is a signal that anger is present. The anger may cross a "trip wire" in your mind that sends anxiety forward to put anger out of your awareness. So often, adult children of narcissists experience tremendous anxiety over repressed feelings that had no place to go when they were younger.

As an exercise, take a moment to identify at least two triggers, both external and internal. Finish the sentence:

I am reacting like this because I believe that _____

_____ will happen.

OR

I am reacting like this because the belief I have about myself is that _____

_____

_____.

For the internal triggers, you can also use this template:

If I allow myself to feel _____

I am most worried that _____

will happen.

OR

If others knew that I felt _____

they would think _____.

◗ EXERCISE: PAST AND FUTURE SELF

When you're feeling stuck in a painful emotion or memory, I'd like to invite you for a moment to write a letter to your past self who was experiencing what you're remembering. Whether or not you've done something like this before, this exercise directly links you to being a compassionate witness for that younger self who didn't have anyone to help her through painful experiences. What would you like that past self to know? And what would that past self most love to hear from you now? Would she like some acknowledgment of what she's feeling? Can you allow her to connect with you and vice versa?

If writing this out doesn't connect with you, simply close your eyes and see your younger self in your mind. Hold her with reverence and imagine that you as an adult are sitting next to her on a park bench, sharing a moment. You might notice some spontaneous images that come to mind, such as her asking you a question or you sharing something with her that makes her laugh. Connect with this younger self and ask her how she would like you to respond to her needs and offer protection? What promise would you like to make to her from this point on?

Some ideas if you get stuck here:

- "I promise to never abandon you."
- "I promise to always hear your feelings with interest."
- "I promise that I will do my very best to meet your needs."
- "You will always have a place within me. You belong."

When your inner child is expressing her feelings to you, what would she most want to hear from you that would honor her feelings? For instance, if she expresses to you that she gets really afraid when you interact with your boss at work, what would you tell her in response? What's available to you now as an adult, that wasn't back then?

If feelings come up that leave you feeling stuck, try out these responses:

- "Of course you're feeling sad when mom ignores you. I'm so sorry that she did that to you. I'm here for you right now and I won't ever abandon you."
- "Would you like me to know how afraid you're feeling right now? I'm listening."
- "Are you feeling angry because what you most need in the entire world is for someone to understand you? I feel angry when someone doesn't understand me too."
- "How can I be of loving support to you now, little one? What would you like for the two of us to do together?
- "How courageous you have been in your life! I feel so proud of you and want you to know that I will always be here to support you."

Of course, not all of us always connect to inner child work, and that's okay. I'd like to normalize this. Try out some of those sample responses above and offer them to yourself as you are in this moment. Tweak some of them to your unique wording and ways of expression and see how they land inside.

Tara Brach, mindfulness teacher and author, offers an exercise for connecting to your future self in her book *Radical Compassion: Learning to Love Yourself and Your World with the Practice of RAIN*, that I will adapt here. Being with our past selves is essential, but we sometimes forget about the future selves waiting for us down the road. This exercise is to forge a connection to the future version of yourself as a way to offer support to you now.

You can do this in written form or simply close your eyes for a moment and settle your body. Take in some deep breaths and let your out-breaths rinse out any accumulated stress or tension. Notice what's happening in your life right now that may be causing some pain, stress, fear, anger, or loneliness. Anything that's causing some kind of tension or reactivity, bring that to your mind. Now look toward the future, say 10, 20, or 30 years down the road.

As you imagine your future self, what do you see her doing? How have all of her life challenges led her to become more wise, humorous, and resilient? You can spend some time defining her in your mind, all the way down to what she's wearing and how she holds herself authentically with others. Bring to mind something that you're currently struggling with and imagine that she, too, is witnessing the struggle. How would your future self respond to what you're experiencing? What would she say to soothe the pain and give you some perspective? In her wisdom, does she remind you that this moment will pass and that life will continue to unfold, with its many peaks and valleys? Or does she validate and honor the feelings you're experiencing, helping you get curious about what they're indicating?

Visualize your future self embracing you as she begins to depart from your mind. Feel her warmth and care connecting with you. Hear her say that you are so not alone in what you're experiencing and that she gets how difficult it is right now. See the twinkle in her eye reflect the years of wisdom she has accumulated. She has your back and is waiting with open arms for you to greet and become her in the future.

What Makes a Healthy Mother?

Healthy mothers are not perfect mothers. They are flawed, imperfect people who are truly doing their best to be available and nurturing to their children. Most of the time, they do all right, and when they screw up, they do their best to make appropriate repairs. A healthy mother is capable of holding space for all of your developmental needs and is flexible when your needs are different from hers. These kinds of mothers generally do not need you to be something that you're not, nor do they need you to take care of them emotionally.

When a mother shows her child that she will be available and present for her, that child develops into a secure individual. Knowing that she is cared for helps her learn how to care for herself. When you're being raised by a narcissistic mother, all of this goes out the window. A narcissistic mother teaches her daughter: *be anything but you*. Mask your feelings of hurt and anger so that I don't have to see them. Deny your needs so that I don't have to meet them. Live an erased life. Maternal narcissism teaches her child that she can be accepted conditionally, rewarding you with "acceptance" for being compliant and agreeable to what she wants. Daughters of narcissists grow themselves around what their mothers need out of fear that they will be rejected, ignored, or abandoned.

In addition, narcissistic mothers may become envious of their daughters and see them as their competitors. One researcher describes the effects of maternal narcissism stating, "to the extent that the mother is unable to facilitate the child's separateness or to encourage the child to move beyond the mother, the child's development is stunted."[42] To put it another way, narcissistic mothers may be best compared to Ursula in *The Little Mermaid*, a sea witch who wants what Ariel has. Through her own narcissistic charm, Ursula convinces Ariel to give up her voice, a major attribute of Ariel's, in favor of being a human, attempting to steal Prince Eric for herself. Adult daughters cope with their mother's jealousy and competition in other ways, but many can relate to the sense that they've somehow signed a contract that permits their mothers to own pieces of them.

Children internalize their parents at very young ages, typically by three to four years old,[43] which means the way they attached to their parents is the way they will attach in other relationships. In addition, the way parents respond to their children is the way their children will respond to themselves throughout the lifespan, unless treated through therapy. Narcissistic mothers instill a kind of insecure attachment that leads their children to experience a lot of anticipatory anxiety about being abandoned or rejected. When daughters grow up and move into other types of relationships, be they romantic or platonic, they carry with them an implicit memory of what a relationship looks like. If their memory could speak, it would sound like, "I have to take care of your needs or you might not like me as I am," or "You might decide to bail, so I'll do whatever it takes to keep you around." If this sounds like you, it's important to gently remind yourself that you, like other human beings, have internalized a type of relationship dynamic. You are not doing anything wrong when you're feeling anxious about being abandoned; rather, you are responding exactly as you learned to in your earlier relationships. Our nervous systems play a powerful role in our psychology in that it is going to react differently depending upon what is considered a threat or not. For someone who has not experienced relational trauma, a relationship may not feel so scary. They may feel generally safe with others and aren't worried about being rejected. For someone who has experienced relational trauma, your nervous system remembers this and will send out a familiar "alert" in the form of anxiety and other physiological responses. Do not be hard on yourself for this, because these responses occur before your conscious mind can get on board. We want our nervous systems to be responding before we can think! Fortunately, with enough awareness, you can begin to help your nervous system register cues of safety so it can be regulated again.

---

42. Marilyn Charles, "Stealing Beauty: An Exploration of Maternal Narcissism," *The Psychoanalytic Review* 88, no. 4 (August, 2001): 549–70, https://doi.org/10.1521/prev.88.4.549.17817.

43. Linda Martinez-Lewi, *Freeing Yourself from the Narcissist in Your Life* (New York: Penguin Publishing Group, 2008), 89.

There is an invitation here, however, that I hope you will take. It is asking you to show care toward the parts of you that internalized a toxic relationship. Your precious body is merely attempting to do its job and still thinks that all relationships will lead to psychological or physical danger. To help our bodies learn that not all relationships will be harmful, we have to start with where we're at. Giving voice to what you're feeling and utilizing curiosity (hello, inner mother!) can be a starting point. Please don't pressure to yourself to "get over it" or white-knuckle your way through pain. How would your inner mother want to respond to those wounds? If you're afraid of abandonment or judgment, how would the inner mother let the afraid part of you know that you are in a different time and place? The early trauma you experienced is over now, but it left very real scars. Bring your attention to what is true in this moment and recognize the story that is being played in your mind. Can you bring yourself out of the traumatic past and back into the present moment? And of course, I so encourage you to engage in therapy with a trauma specialist who can really help guide you through those experiences safely.

Now, let's return to the relationship that you internalized. So often, adult daughters can feel defeated by the sense that all relationships are dangerous, as if some invisible force prevents them from responding differently. Let's walk through what happens so you can track the experience. You'll likely feel triggered when something within your relationship reminds you of an experience you had with your mother. You may be consciously aware of the trigger, but likely it will be an unconscious reaction. Old survival mechanisms may rise up to shield you from the pain and pull your awareness away to something else. Daughters end up feeling as though they are doomed to this fate forever, but they are not. If you can, I'd like to invite you to show compassion toward yourself for this pattern, the way you might to a dear friend.

Begin by taking in a slow and deep breath. Place your hand over your heart and gently acknowledge what is causing you pain, whatever it may be. You might say to yourself, "This is a painful feeling and memory. I have a desire to want to get away from it and bury myself in a distraction. If I need to, I'll allow myself to do that, but if I can, I'm going to try and be welcoming toward myself as I sit in this experience." Self-compassion does not need to sound flowery or be eloquent either. It could sound as simple as, "This sucks. I hope I can get through this right now." And the thing about compassion is that you don't have to *do* anything to be deserving of it. You already are.

If you're aware that you've been triggered, investigate the trigger with curiosity. Can you show yourself some kindness? You might say, "No wonder I'm feeling anxious right now. It's hard for me to feel safe when my spouse is away," or "Of course it's going to be hard for me to unwind when my nervous system is activated like this." Talk to yourself from the heart.

Avoid using judging, blaming, or guilt-inducing language. Honor the feeling that is present by asking if there is a need longing to be met. "I am feeling aggravated and a little sleepy right now. Do I feel this way because my need for rest is not being met?"

Becoming Your Own Advocate

Many of us live our lives in a state of disconnection. Sometimes we do this consciously, such as when we're having a bad day and we zone out on social media; other times we do it unconsciously. This state of disconnection that we all fall victim to doesn't need to be judged or criticized, merely recognized, so that we can choose whether or not to stay disconnected or reconnect to ourselves. In her book *I Know I'm in There Somewhere*, Helene Brenner describes this process of disconnection as being a byproduct of women being conditioned to "over-respond." Brenner states, "when women lose themselves in connection, when they no longer see their selves in the mirror, they begin to reject or ignore who they truly are in favor of who they are supposed to be."[44]

It is not uncommon for most of us to have different versions of ourselves that we show to others. Your evening Netflix-watching self is going to look and act very differently from your work-life self. It's still you, just in different contexts. If you can be different versions of yourself, the question then becomes, who is this Self underneath? Who is the Self experiencing life as it unfolds? Yes, your outer self will look different, but your inner Self remains relatively unchanged.

Ask a teacher, a philosopher, a guru, and a therapist to describe the concept of *Self* and you'll likely get four different answers. Yet most of the definitions have a unifying theme binding them together. I believe the Self is the part of us that is able to witness everything, all from a place of curiosity, compassion, awareness, and non-judgment. Some people describe accessing *Self* when they're engaged in meditation or instances when they suddenly have an acute awareness of the present moment. When we're connected to Self, our responses to what we're experiencing will look different from when we're disconnected from our feelings or stuck in old survival mechanisms that block us off from reality.

The Self does not discriminate against particular "negative" feelings or thoughts, nor is it a place where only "positive" thoughts or feelings exist. The Self just witnesses. When we're fused with a particular thought or feeling, we feel that we *are* that thought or feeling. There's no separation. When we're in Self, however, we recognize a thought or feeling for what it is:

---

44. Helene Brenner, *I Know I'm in There Somewhere: A Woman's Guide to Finding Her Inner Voice and Living a Life of Authenticity* (New York: Gotham Books, 2004), 25-26.

a passing state. It's not uncommon for people to feel particularly wary of their emotions, like grief or anger, in which the common worry is that they will be labeled as "an angry person" or "weak." I've had clients tell me, "I'm not an angry person," to which I would respond, "Of course you're not. You are not a fearful, happy, or sad person either. But you have the capacity to *feel* angry, afraid, happy, and sad." This distinction is important. Our feelings do not define who we are but they can be informers of what we are needing moment to moment.

Our feelings are like weather systems and the Self is the sky. We would never say the sky is rain, but we would say "it's raining today." Depending on the season or time of day, the sky is going to look different and varied. No weather condition is permanent. The sky holds all kinds of interesting elements: clouds, rain, thunder and lightning, stars, comets, hues of blue, violet, pink, and deep night. The Self is no different. It is a host to all of our passing emotions, thoughts, and impulses. We are not a fixed state, but capable of experiencing a range of feeling and thought.

How do we get to Self? Anything that taps us into a natural state of curiosity, compassion, awareness, and non-judgment, of noticing what is happening moment to moment, is a stepping-stone. Meditation, for instance, allows us to practice witnessing our thoughts and focusing on breath to anchor us into the present moment. Within this practice, you can observe yourself from a nonjudgmental lens. Playing, being creative, and engaging in movement are also ways in which we might access Self. In my own clinical work, I've found that the more an individual is able to access Self when they're experiencing distressing feelings, allowing the feelings to be there, the more likely those feelings will pass. Ironically, leaning into the experience by just noticing deactivates its intensity and alleviates the tension more quickly than techniques like avoidance, thinking happy thoughts, or forcing a different perspective.

In Tara Brach's book *Radical Compassion: Learning to Love Yourself and Your World with the Practice of R.A.I.N.*, she tells a beautiful story from the Buddhist lineage that illustrates the concept of the Self underneath the thoughts. She tells the story of Buddhist monks who had to relocate their beloved large clay Buddha statue due to construction. The monks revered this statue and sought the help of a large crane to move it. When the crane began to lift the statue, the clay began to crack and as a means of preservation, the statue was put back down and covered in a tarp so that the oncoming storm wouldn't damage it.

During the storm, one of the monks went to check on the covered Buddha to make sure it was preserved and noticed a light shining through one of the cracks. A curious thing, the monk alerted the others to come and inspect, and soon enough they were chipping away at the clay.

When they were done, they discovered that underneath, the Buddha was covered in gold. This clay covering had been preserving the gold underneath.[45]

We can think of the golden Buddha as the Self within all of us. Despite our clay coverings, there is gold underneath. Even when you cannot access Self, trust that its golden presence is there. The Self is very similar to the inner mother. Both of these forces are capable of witnessing and being *with*. When we're in pain, the Self or inner mother, whichever you get to first, can help you take an eagle-eye view of your experience, an approach that naturally creates more compassion and understanding than when you're fused with it. Zooming out the lens helps us take in more of the landscape surrounding any situation and perhaps allows us to see things from a different perspective.

◗◖ EXERCISE: PAUSE

As an exercise to help you defuse from a distressing experience, I'd like for you to PAUSE. This approach may help you to "zoom out," so to speak, and recognize for a moment what is happening both internally and externally. When we PAUSE, we are not checking out or moving away from painful experiences, rather we are taking a moment to notice what is feeding our current state of mind and gently connecting back to Self.

P: Pause what you're doing and take three deep breaths in and out, releasing a little more air in the out-breath.

A: Assess what is happening. Name the facts (i.e., "I'm at work," "I have a lot of paperwork to do," "I need to eat," or "I'm with my partner in the car.")

U: Understand. Provide understanding toward the part of you that is experiencing distress with thoughts like, "It's okay to feel this way. This is hard right now. All you have to do is be."

S: Story. What is the story happening in your mind? In what ways is the story missing information? Is the story being driven by anxious thoughts or factual evidence? Can you add more to the story to give it more context? How would the story sound if you infused it with compassion or self-empathy?

E: Emotions. Name the emotions you're feeling right now. Ask them what they are trying to tell you about what you are needing in this moment.

---

45. Tara Brach, *Radical Compassion: Learning to Love Yourself and Your World with the Practice of R.A.I.N.* (New York: Penguin Random House, 2019), 33-34.

Chapter 4

LETTING YOUR NEEDS AND VALUES LEAD THE WAY

We all come into this world needing. As infants, our basic needs include nourishment, physical safety, including shelter, and emotional attunement from our mothers. As we get older, our needs change. Toddlers, for instance, are enamored with their need to be autonomous. They want to get into everything and are fascinated by the world around them. As we move into adolescence, our need to fit in, be different, and belong to our friend groups takes precedence. In adulthood, all of those needs remain, though to varying degrees. In our relationships, we may crave mutuality and respect, for instance, and when these needs go unmet, we feel an emotion like frustration, anger, or sadness to alert us.

Many of us tend to perceive our needs as being solely related to physical survival. When you go to the store and think about buying an expensive bottle of wine or specialty food, you might wonder, "Do I really need this?" Or perhaps at one point in your life you said, "I need," and then someone jumped in to remind you that what you "need" is more about what you "want." We equate a want with something we can go without and a need with survival. However, if we look at needs and wants from the lens of how it might enhance our lives or make an experience more meaningful, we might discover a different answer. I would argue that wants and needs do not need to be mutually exclusive, which is a radical concept for most. When I want something, say a beautifully knitted sweater, I'm responding to my need to feel warm and comfortable. If this sweater is outside of my price range, for instance, I might recognize that my need to feel warm and comfortable could be met in another way or with a more affordable item. Wants can be thought of as an opening into witnessing our deeper needs.

Adult daughters of narcissists have been programmed to ignore and dismiss their needs. This can lead to daughters experiencing an inner conflict between a part of them that has needs and a part that has been conditioned to bypass those needs. Narcissistic mothers make it clear to their daughters, in some form or another, that their needs don't matter. To remedy this, daughters learn to live a partial life, where their needs come last or go unattended for years. Many of the adult daughters I have worked with describe feeling guilt for asking for what they need or even acknowledging that they have a need in the first place. These women are no stranger to living "comfortably" in scarcity. They become more like stagehands in their relationships, giving the main actors what they need while they themselves remain hidden in shadow.

Marshall Rosenberg, founder of the Center for Nonviolent Communication, defines needs as "resources that life requires in order to sustain itself."[46] Needs are not limited to our physical wellbeing, although that is included, but encompass all aspects of our selfhood: spirituality, emotional wellbeing, mental clarity, community, relationship, autonomy, and connection. Needs are foundational to our total wellbeing.

When our needs are met, we generally feel a sense of contentedness and security. When our needs go unmet, are ignored, denied, or unseen, we will feel uneasy, agitated, irritable, and restless. Emotions that are typically described as "negative" will present themselves when a need is not being fulfilled. The good news, however, is that those negative feelings are actually our friends. They are telling us something important about ourselves and what we need. Rosenberg and other teachers of nonviolent communication have a lovely way of putting this together that I'll reference below. Typically, this is used for communicating our needs to another person, but I like to use it to communicate my needs to myself as well.

(Your name)_____, are you feeling

_____ because you need (or because

what is most important to you is) _____

and you'd really like _____ right now?

---

46. Marshall Rosenberg, *Living Nonviolent Communication: Practical Tools to Connect and Communicate Skillfully in Every Situation* (Louisville: Sounds True, 2012), 2–3.

It might look like this: Hannah, are you feeling sad because you need connection right now and you'd really like some conversation?

Try it out yourself this week. Here is a list of universal needs to get acquainted with. You'll typically find that when you are experiencing an unpleasant emotion, that's an indicator that a need is not being fulfilled. These feelings are letting you know something important. Consider your feelings as your closest allies rushing forward to make sure you are getting exactly what you need.

Connection		**Honesty**	**Meaning**
acceptance	stability	authenticity	awareness
affection	support	integrity	celebration of life
appreciation	to know and be	presence	challenge
belonging	known		clarity
cooperation	to see and be seen	**Play**	competence
communication	to understand and	joy	consciousness
closeness	be understood	humor	contribution
community	trust		creativity
companionship	warmth	**Peace**	discovery
compassion		beauty	efficacy
consideration	**Physical**	communion	effectiveness
consistency	**Well-Being**	ease	growth
empathy	air	equality	hope
inclusion	food	harmony	learning
intimacy	movement/exercise	inspiration	mourning
love	rest/sleep	order	participation
mutuality	sexual expression		purpose
nurturing	safety	**Autonomy**	self-expression
respect/self-respect	shelter	choice	stimulation
safety	touch	freedom	to matter
security	water	independence	understanding
		space	
		spontaneity	

Essentially, from this place of being synchronized with our feelings and needs we can know ourselves fully in each moment. Similar to how a plant intuitively expands itself toward the sun and then contracts in relation to the moon's energy, we too expand and contract depending upon our specific needs. Our feelings in each moment shape and shift in response to whether or not our needs are being met. Having a feeling isn't the same thing as acting out a feeling. For instance, if your need for play and relaxation was disrupted by a disgruntled family member, you may notice yourself feeling anger. The feeling of anger as it arises in your body isn't a problem. It only becomes problematic when we take that anger and use it to lash out at someone or turn it back on ourselves. The feeling will naturally remit when we show an interest in it and use it toward adaptively responding to our need that isn't being fulfilled.

What is lovely about practicing nonviolent communication is that invites us to approach all needs as being important. There's no such thing as a need that is lesser. In the book *Living Nonviolent Communication: Practical Tools to Connect and Communicate Skillfully in Every Situation*, Rosenberg states that expressing our needs and learning to hear the needs of others "shows us how to express what is alive in us and to see what is alive in other people."[47]

For daughters of narcissistic mothers, the practice of expressing what is alive in them was not tolerated. Narcissists are extremely fragile, and other people's needs and emotions will likely feel threatening to their sense of self. As a daughter of a narcissist, your "aliveness" was not seen or responded to in the way you most needed. Elsa Ronningstam, who has been referenced earlier, reminds us that inside a narcissist is a swirl of fragility ranging from "vulnerable self-esteem, perfectionism, feelings of inferiority, chronic envy, shame and rage, feelings of boredom and emptiness, hypervigilance, and affective reactivity."[48] Your needs were like little paper cuts to your mother, and every time you expressed them, she felt "cut" by their presence. If you were lucky, some of your needs could get met in a sideways fashion, as long as she could benefit from it.

Daniel Shaw, whom we met in chapter two, describes how children relate to a "traumatizing narcissist"[49] by either developing their own inner persecutor or disavowing their needs completely. The inner persecutor, which Shaw refers to as the persecutor/protector, tells them "it's too dangerous to expose yourself, be nothing, and have no hope."[50] This internal mechanism begins like any survival strategy: for protection. You can see how a daughter might develop her own inner persecutor out of a need to protect herself from venturing too far into a dangerous territory. I have heard individuals describe their inner persecutor as a mechanism that attacks them first, before anyone else can. In a sense, it feels protective, but

---

47. Rosenberg, *Living Nonviolent Communication,* location 54 of 3894.
48. Elsa Ronningstam, "Narcissistic Personality Disorder: A Clinical Perspective," *The Journal of Psychiatric Practice* 17, no. 2 (2011): 90, https://doi.org/10.1097/01.pra.0000396060.67150.40.
49. Shaw, *Traumatic Narcissism,* 12.
50. Shaw, *Traumatic Narcissism,* 8.

of course leaves many scars. The other protective mechanism is one where the child, and later the adult, disavows their needs completely by seeing them as unnecessary, externalizing them onto others (i.e. "I'm not the one with needs, you are").[51] Shaw refers to this as the externalizing mechanism (i.e., "I'm not the one with needs, you are"). These adults sadly exhibit many narcissistic traits and behaviors themselves and may even view other people's needs as weaknesses, leading them to leave a life of bitterness and loneliness.

According to Shaw, the traumatizing narcissist diminishes and suppresses the subjectivity of the other person. They want one subjective viewpoint to dominate: theirs. When narcissistic mothers can manipulate their daughters out of their own subjective experiences, their daughters inevitably wind up feeling confusion and self-doubt.[52] If you've struggled with the self-doubt monster, know that this is a byproduct of being raised by a narcissist. The way out of this is by recognizing the self-doubt for what it is: a mirage that is deeply misleading. When you are experiencing self-doubt, what this really translates to is a lack of *self-trust*. Self-trust is an ever-evolving practice that we must engage with over and over again until it becomes natural and second-nature. I would almost encourage you to do the opposite of what your toxic doubt is telling you. If doubt says "you probably shouldn't ask for that," then you say "too bad! I'm going to ask anyway."

Adults whose needs were chronically undermet in childhood may approach relationships already denying their needs out of habit. The association is made that having needs in relationships will only lead to hurt and disappointment, so individuals learn to suppress their needs and keep them out of view. Adults who internalized their mother's rejection of their needs to the point of developing their own narcissistic defenses may experience profound deficits in their emotional and interpersonal lives. These individuals may use the externalizing defense Shaw described, in which they disavow their needs and relate to the needs of others as less than.

Self-trust comes about when we can know and respond to what we feel and need without being impeded by guilt or shame.

One signal that our needs are not getting met may be anger.

Cara, a 28-year-old interior designer, told me once how she recognized that anger (she referred to it as "my winged dragon") often roared overhead to signal that "mom was on her throne and waging war on the peasants" (i.e., herself and her two sisters). When she was a child, she would imagine her winged dragon swooping her up and taking her somewhere

---

51. Shaw, *Traumatic Narcissism, 8.*
52. Shaw, *Traumatic Narcissism, 12.*

BREAK FREE FROM NARCISSISTIC MOTHERS

else if need be. Even as a small child, she was aware of this hugely important emotion and what it was signaling: "I don't like this. Get out of here."

Through our work together, Cara eventually came to recognize and respect her anger for what it was: A signal that something didn't feel safe, healthy, or right. However, one day she noticed a smaller version of her fiery friend, but found herself perplexed by its visit. "I was at home and my wife was cooking dinner. It was quiet and nothing stood out to me as requiring my anger, but here it was."

"Did anything happen before that triggered this feeling?" I wondered.

"No, that's the funny thing. I couldn't figure it out!" She said.

"Well, I wonder if we might take a moment to inquire with this anger if a need isn't being met?"

Cara closed her eyes and paused for a moment. Suddenly I saw tears streaming down her face. She opened her eyes and revealed that a need for connection with her wife wasn't being met.

"I realized that for the past two weeks we kind of got caught in this rhythm of busyness that didn't give us any time to just connect. When she was in the kitchen, I felt her absence, and as I'm saying that out loud I'm realizing how much I miss her." Cara was making an important connection with her anger, and when we invited her to inquire into her needs, she found the link.

I responded with, "You were looking for something external and obvious to understand your anger, and isn't that so normal? So many of us forget to go inward and check out if a need is not being met. We so often end up looking outside of ourselves that we overlook our own ecosystem of needs. How is it for us to be noticing your need for connection together?"

Cara shared, "It feels really good to be able to have language for what's going on beneath my anger. I had been conditioned to be on the lookout for my mom's very obvious behaviors and that angry dragon got very good at intercepting. Now it's still there, looking out for me, but I've been quicker to question its validity when I don't see tangible signs to respond to. I don't want to keep pushing it away when the trigger is less obvious. I see now where it is telling me about my needs."

For the next couple of sessions, Cara and I kept a steady presence in her house of needs, and worked on enhancing her "needs literacy"[53] so that she could learn to hear their call for attention.

A common refrain in nonviolent communication, which we'll address in a moment, is that needs are not strategies.[54] For instance, Cara had a need for connection. If we hadn't mined her inner self to guide us to this conclusion, she might have focused on the strategy (without realizing her need in the first place), such as sulking until her wife noticed her; going out for a drink; questioning her relationship, wondering if it was right for her; or demanding that her wife change. These responses would have likely led to tension between her and her beloved, which would have been counterintuitive to meeting her need.

A *strategy* is how we get or achieve something; a *need* is without strategy. It either exists or it doesn't. When we communicate our strategy to someone, we lose a valuable opportunity to identify and express a need. All needs are universal;[55] all strategies are not. If we tell a partner "I want you to listen to me," that is a strategy. A need might sound like this: "When you get on your phone when I'm talking to you about something painful, it makes me feel sad because my need to be seen isn't being met. Would you be willing to put your phone down while I talk to you?"

Many of us haven't learned how to identify or express our needs. Sadly, this deficit causes great distress in our important relationships, and we end up tangled in a spider's web of confusion. In narcissistic homes, this confusion gets amplified. Narcissistic mothers make their life's work about keeping their needs met above all else. Their tactics of grinding you down, causing you to doubt yourself and question your own inner knowing creates a kind of wasteland. This apocalyptic space allows for nothing within it to grow or be harvested. Your needs wither like a plant without water, and you soon learn to live without them.

Learning to Meet Your Needs

Fortunately, we can re-wild this inner landscape to allow for all variety of needs to coexist. We start by identifying the many universal needs we all share with one another. Then we go into looking at how our feelings can guide us toward meeting those needs.

Use language that moves you toward your needs, not away from them. In other words, state what you need. As simple as this may be, you may notice how much more practiced you are

---

53. Rosenberg, *Living Nonviolent Communication*, 4.
54. Rosenberg, *Living Nonviolent Communication*, 2.
55. Rosenberg, *Living Nonviolent Communication*, 154.

BREAK FREE FROM NARCISSISTIC MOTHERS

at saying what you don't need. This is common among adult daughters who learned to please others and so *begin their need statements with a deficit so as not to impose.*

Anemic needs statements might sound like the following:

- "I don't need a lot of time, but could you..."
- "It's not a big deal if I don't get this, but maybe I could..."
- "I don't want to be so flustered all the time."
- "I want to stop feeling less-than in my career."
- "It's important that I stop procrastinating."

Why am I calling those need statements anemic? They are telling us what you don't want, rather than what you do. Marshall Rosenberg says it another way: "If we just tell ourselves what we don't want to do, we're not likely to make much change in the situation."[56]

Let's take the above anemic statements and polish them up so they reveal and connect us to the underlying need in a declarative way. In positive language, it might sound like:

- "Would you be willing to spare 15 minutes? I'd like to talk with you about..."
- "What I would really love more of is..."
- "I am longing for more inner peace and resilience."
- "What would restore my sense of contribution to my career is the ability to get a certification."
- "I would really like to create more time to engage in what's important to me."

In nonviolent communication (NVC), the path recommended is one in which all parties' needs are met to their complete satisfaction, rather than forming compromises.[57] With adult daughters of narcissists, I am going to recommend a slightly different path. Given that you have spent most of your life trying to meet your mother's needs to no avail, I am going to suggest that this practice be about making your needs clearer and more real to you. This goes against the premise of NVC in one major way: it keeps the focus exclusively on you rather than on meeting both your and your mother's needs. You are always welcome to try true NVC with others in your life, but I caution you to beware of using it with your mother, as her narcissism may poison the well from which you're trying to give.

I've taken some of the nonviolent communication principles and changed them a bit so that the focus remains on your needs. Narcissists are most of the time (if not always) unable to

---

56. Rosenberg, *Living Nonviolent Communication,* 13.
57. Rosenberg, *Living Nonviolent Communication,* 2.

engage with the mutuality that is part of NVC. Owing to their own wounding, their ability to understand your needs is going to be exquisitely rare.

Since this book is about healing you, this is where we must begin. To know what we need, it's important we know what we feel, which is our starting point.

1. Sense your own needs underlying your emotions. This might look like "I feel a little tense. I didn't get any sleep and I'm a little wound up. I think I feel some sadness. I am needing rest and quiet time."

2. Express your needs first and foremost to yourself: "I am noticing that I have a need for play today."

3. Be compassionate with yourself: "This practice is really hard for me to do. I'm worried I'm not getting it right. My compassionate self wants to remind me that it's okay to not have all the answers yet."

4. Check in and see how that need could be fulfilled: "Since I am needing rest and my family is at home being loud, I think the best way for me to secure some rest is to ask if they would be willing to speak at a lower volume while I take a nap."

5. Begin to explore strategies and actions that could meet your needs to your satisfaction. What are you requesting from yourself or others? Perhaps you're recognizing that a request to your spouse for some time together is in order. Or maybe you're noticing how deeply your need for independence is and are wanting to request space from your roommate.

6. Try out one of these strategies. Don't worry about getting it right, just move toward what you're needing.

7. Notice if that need feels satisfied. If not, how can you move closer to satisfying it?

To summarize, you start by identifying the emotion that might be alerting you to an unfulfilled need, then you put a name to the need. Then you identify the strategy that would best meet your need. If you are asking for a need to be met by or with another human, frame the strategy as a request in positive action language. Meaning, ask for what you want in the clearest way, not what you don't want. Move away from words that create vagueness and instead make your request explicit. Rosenberg really emphasizes the importance of requesting of others rather than demanding. A request makes room for the other person to say no (and also respond with their needs), whereas a demand does not.

⟩◖ EXERCISE: NEEDS AND STRATEGIES

If you have a need for quiet in a very busy home and you tell your children, "I need you guys to stop making so much noise for an hour," notice how restricting that is. Are you requesting or are you demanding? Are you telling your children what you want or what you don't want? Let's take the above principles and apply them to this scenario.

We've identified the need: for quiet, which if we take that a step further may also satisfy a need for self-reflection, giving you a sense of peace, and clarity.

What are some strategies to get this need met? Write your own. I'll list a few examples down below. Remember, strategies aren't needs: They are merely the ways in which we move toward our needs.

- Ask the children to be quiet for 30 minutes.
- Leave to go for a walk.
- Unplug the television.
- Have the children go outside for 30 minutes.
- Put the kids in time-out.

My strategies for quiet and self-reflection:

How can you put the need and strategy into a request that honors both your need and their need? "I am feeling very tired and need some quiet. Would you three be willing to keep your voices lower and play together outside for the next 30 minutes?" How would you frame your needs using a request?

What is lovely about nonviolent communication are the principles guiding it. Rosenberg states, "This approach to communication emphasizes compassion—rather than fear, guilt, shame, blame, coercion, or threat of punishment—as the motivation for action. In other words, it is about getting what we want for reasons that we will not regret later."[58]

---

58. Rosenberg, *Living Nonviolent Communication*, location 127 of 3894.

Being able to state what one wants or needs in a way that reduces regret later is a key piece in communicating from a place of empowerment and clarity. I have witnessed how some adult daughters feel regretful after they lashed out at their mothers or shut down during an opportunity to set a boundary. We can mitigate this regret by learning how to speak our needs from a place of integrity. We can also apply the above strategy to how we respond to our own needs. Inquiring within and having a dialogue with parts of ourselves is a wonderful way to assess how we're doing. For adult daughters, the ability to notice feelings, name needs, and respond to these forces is essential. Of all the various forms healing takes, knowing what our feelings are, what they're telling us, and what their connection is to how our needs are getting fulfilled or not, may be the most necessary piece of recovery.

I wish to invite you into a space with yourself where all of your needs can be seen as opportunities to respond to yourself from a place of care. No need is too much in this space. No need is too small either. All needs are valid as they are. You needn't waste precious energy explaining them or justifying their existence. They simply are.

Tragic Expressions of Unmet Needs

In *Nonviolent Communication*, Marshall Rosenberg describes an individual's hostile, judgmental, violent, or abusive actions as "tragic expressions of unmet needs."[59] What makes these behaviors tragic is that they never allow the person to get their original need met. You may have seen these tragic expressions manifest in situations like customer service, either from your own experience or witnessing it from others. A patron at a restaurant berates the server for the food taking longer than they would like. Their need to get nourishment is not being met and tragically, they verbally assault the service staff in the hope that this will get their need met. Would you want someone in charge of your food to be put in a position to feel extreme fear, guilt, or anger toward you? Likely not.

Here's another example: You get into an argument with a spouse or partner and call them an "asshole," when really you'd like to find a way to get closer to them so that your need for connection could be met. When our attempts at meeting our needs come with violence of any kind, it is going to cause pain and disconnection.

Your mother's narcissism is a tragic expression of significant unmet needs. However, it is not your job to meet those needs for her. Not only is it impossible to do, but your attempts will reinforce the non-mutual, toxic dynamic of the relationship, putting you right back in a role you are working so hard to step out of. When she becomes highly critical of you, or

---

59. Rosenberg, *Living Nonviolent Communication*, 7.

brushes your needs off like a fleck of dust, recognize that all of those behaviors—whether they're macro or micro—are tragic expressions of unmet needs. She doesn't have the language to express herself adequately, nor is she able to hear your needs without making them about her. When she hears your needs as criticisms or rejections of her, she is inviting you to enact her early trauma, with you as the "all-bad" other, and with her as "all-good" victim.

Your mother's judgments of you don't actually have anything to do with you, but it's easy to hear them that way. You were taught to bear the responsibility for meeting her needs and easing her feelings, not the other way around. As a child, the fear of losing your mother outweighed your needs for things like authenticity and freedom, so naturally you gave those up. As an adult, however, if you continue to take ownership of her needs and feelings, making them your responsibility, then her narcissism triumphs and she stays comfortable in her belief that others are responsible for her. Essentially you wind up holding onto something that doesn't belong to you. Without meaning to, you become a thief. Give her feelings and needs back to her where they belong!

If you can begin practicing hearing your mother's attacks as tragic expressions of unmet needs (that you are *not* going to take on), then you no longer have to hear them as judgments of *you*. And when you are free from making her words mean something about you, when you can extradite yourself from that prison, you will find liberation. Of course, it's not as simple as flipping a switch where suddenly you are no longer affected. You will feel the effects of her words and judgments of you because you are human, but my hope is that you will no longer internalize her words or relate to them as truth. They are not.

I'd like to take a moment to emphasize something important about receiving verbal attacks— abusive language—or experiencing physical acts of violence against your body. It is perfectly okay for you to remove yourself from any situation that feels unsafe. You are not required to be the bigger person and "tough it out." Please allow yourself to leave any situation that does not feel good for you to be in. Sometimes in this work, individuals mistakenly believe that they ought to find "inner strength" and be stoic in the face of abusive behavior from their mothers. Please remember to listen to your needs and your feelings when you are in a situation like this. They will not be telling you to stay and "be strong," but will likely want you to leave and protect yourself.

If you find yourself in an exchange with your mother where she is teetering on the ledge of behaving in a way that is unhealthy for you, yet you feel safe enough to state your boundaries and intentions, you might try something like, "I'm going to have to end this conversation right now. I will call you next week." And that's it. There's no requirement that you offer a lengthy explanation full of qualifications. Let yourself off the hook, state a simple boundary or need, and exit the situation (or change the topic, talk to another family member nearby, step outside to make a call, or extricate yourself from the situation in some other way).

What's important to recognize here is that your mother will likely continue to see your needs as less important than her own. It's difficult for her to accept the fact that you are completely separate from her. Daniel Shaw describes this relationship, stating, "The traumatizing narcissistic parent sees only her own needs as valid—and characterizes the child who tries to express her needs as needy, selfish, and dependent. At the same time, the traumatizing narcissist parent cannot bear the possibility of being surpassed and not needed by the child, and so must undermine the child's efforts toward independence."[60]

As the daughter of a narcissistic mother, you were caught in a trap. On the one hand, you were told that your needs for dependence, care, and support were selfish, which pushed you into a place of low self-worth and chronic self-doubt. Then, when you attempted to find your own way, build your sense of self, and pave a path forward, you were told that you couldn't hack it, or that you were "making a big deal out of nothing." In the latter case, you may have also been told, in a punishing voice, that your efforts were going to fail anyway. In some ways, your succeeding might have felt like a betrayal against your mother, and your desire to be independent was also seen as wrong and selfish.[61]

Within your mother's narcissistic relationship, you simply were not entitled to need, separate, fail, succeed, grow, or surpass her.[62] Fortunately, you are no longer obligated to meet the requirements of that system. As you dissolve your contract with your mother, you'll likely find some mental and emotional scars that you've endured from living with a narcissist. It's vital we treat those scars with care and respect. Scars, like ancient ruins of battles long past, remain as a site we show great reverence to, for they reveal our resilience. Where there is a scar, there is healing. What makes a scar is the healing energy the body generates to mend the wound. Remember that this healing energy lives within you. You don't even need to do anything to activate it, as it is an automatic response that comes when we're wounded. Your own healing energy can also be enhanced through self-compassion and learning to rewrite your inner narrative.

Your thinking mind is a powerhouse of perception. We can easily get caught up in the story of our minds, relating to the narrative as though it were true without considering other possibilities. It's not the thoughts themselves that are problematic, but in how we relate to them. Could you imagine what would happen if we all believed what our thoughts were saying all the time? We wouldn't be able to get much done, let alone have any time to be functional. Of

60. Shaw, *Traumatic Narcissism,* 35.
61. Shaw, *Traumatic Narcissism,* 34–35.
62. Shaw, *Traumatic Narcissism,* 35.

course, there are going to be instances where your thoughts will be pretty benign, such as "I need to go to the post office," which won't pose much of a problem. The type of thoughts that require a new kind of relating to are the ones that say things like "you're a massive failure," or "no one is going to like you," or "that was such a stupid thing to say." Since those types of thoughts feel threatening, we end up giving them more attention than their benign counterparts. What I'd like for you to consider is to start relating to those thoughts as false narrative, something that is not based on fact, but fear. As a miniature thought experiment, I'd like to invite you to check in with your body when your mind generates unhelpful and devaluing thoughts against you and, conversely, what happens when you bring in compassion toward yourself.

◗◖ EXERCISE: BODY CHECK-IN

What do you notice happening in your body right now?

....

....

....

What happens in your body when you read these thoughts?

- "You'll never get this right."
- "Wow, that really was dumb of me."
- "It's too hard. I should just quit."
- "No one cares what I have to say."

....

....

....

Name how your perception of yourself changes:

....

....

....

Identify the emotions that came up:

....

....

....

Describe the behaviors you might have engaged in after hearing these thoughts (i.e., lying around, hiding in the bathroom, shutting down):

....

....

....

What happens in your body when you relate to those thoughts through the lens of self-compassion?

- "It's okay to fail. We just get up and try again."
- "Woo, that was hard! I've got this."
- "Today is really hard, but I'm going to take it one step at a time."
- "I took in a false message about what other people think of me. Not everyone is my mom. Plus, most people are pretty generous."

....

....

....

Name how your perception of yourself changes:

....

....

....

Identify the emotions that came up:

....

....

....

Describe the behaviors you might have engaged in after hearing these thoughts (i.e., taking in a deep breath, going for a walk, calling a supportive friend, smiling):

....

....

....

How Needs Become Needy

As an adult daughter of a narcissist, you are all too familiar with the theme of your needs being needy and selfish. If you were the scapegoat of your family system, then you know this theme acutely. If you're unfamiliar with where the term *scapegoat* comes from, it was an ancient practice among communities in which a goat representing the sins of the community was sacrificed to symbolize renewal. Being the family scapegoat means that you take on the blame for everyone, serving as a metaphorical sacrificial goat for the family. However, you needn't be a scapegoat to experience this. Daughters who were considered the golden child, family mascot, or even the lost child will experience their mother's blame, ridicule, and gaslighting, just in a different way.[63] The labels don't really matter; the effects of maternal narcissism are still the same.

---

63 Hall, *The Narcissist in Your Life*, 181.

When you take a risk and step out of whatever role you had to play and start to honor your needs, securing healthy boundaries, or cutting off contact, you will inevitably come up against that old ghost of guilt, the one that has been haunting you for most of your life. Within that ghost story lies the narrative that you are hurting your mother when you start to separate from her. You were told that having needs makes you needy or selfish, so you become the "all-bad" daughter for daring to put yourself first.

When you sacrificed your needs in service of putting your mother's before yours, you became the "all-good" daughter, reinforcing the belief that being selfless is ideal. However, this came at a huge cost. In order to play the game, you had to leave yourself behind. The price for admission is to deny your needs and treat your emotions as intrusions on other people's lives.

The all-good or all-bad paradigm was reinforced by your mother unconsciously (and sometimes consciously), as narcissism is literally a split within the self. There's no space for a middle ground to exist. Buried under her façade is a deeply entrenched fear that she is not good enough either. She passed this belief onto you, unconsciously relating to you as though you were not good enough. This was how she attempted to shield herself from her own sense of deficiency: by projecting it onto you. Relating to you as though you were the one who was failing and not living up to expectations gave her someone outside of herself to be abusive toward. Your needs became you being needy; your right for self-care became selfish. As a human being, it is your right to have needs! In fact, it's unavoidable. Can you see how using the word *needy* might be used as an attempt to convince you that having needs is wrong?

❑ EXERCISE: "NEEDY" VS. "NEEDS"

When you hear "needy" what image comes to mind? What happens in your body as you connect to that word?

What about if we remove the "y" from that word and simply say "having needs." What comes up now for you?

You might notice a stronger sense of conviction, of rightness, that yes, having needs is part of the deal of being a human. You may also be aware of a familiar thread of disgust and wrongness underlying this, making it hard to integrate the logical knowing that needs are important.

What would it take for you to move closer to the part of you that can recognize that having needs is allowed and right?

Your mother's narcissism has likely perverted your healthy experience of needs, self-care, and boundaries and turned them into words like needy, selfish, mean, or egotistical. How terribly sad that something as healthy and normal as having needs was made out to be such a burden for you.

Can we change that now?

What happens if your needs are given the attention they deserve? How might life change for you?

What makes self-care and boundaries so important to human life?

Consider for a moment of all the ways in which humans and non-humans have needs in order to function properly.

- What happens when a car goes too long without being driven or having its oil changed?
- What is the result of a computer with too many apps going at once?
- When a baby doesn't get enough rest, what's likely to happen?
- If you have children of your own, what happens when their need for play doesn't get met?
- When an animal goes without food or water, what happens?
- What happens if your need to share your feelings with significant others gets thwarted?

As you can likely see, when human and non-human needs are not being met, it causes a problem. You are no different. Your needs for play, rest, nourishment, connection with others, nature, movement, and authenticity (the list goes on), are so important that denying them can lead to significant challenges in your life. When we're living outside of our needs, we are more likely to feel anxious, depressed, low-energy, unmotivated, and burned out. As part of your healing journey, I wish to offer you a prescription that reads: must meet needs daily.

Values

This leads us into the discussion of values and how they propel us toward living a more meaningful life. Being in touch with our values and living in accordance with them is like having a compass that tells us if we're going in the right direction. Values are different from goals. Both have significance and both are important to be in touch with, as they offer us a connection to what we want in life. The major difference between a value and a goal is that a goal ends, whereas a value is never ending. What I love about values is that they are always available for us to strive toward. There's not an end goal to our values, merely a continuous unfolding of a path toward greater life meaning and fulfillment.

Values and needs often intersect, so you may discover that one of your universal needs is also one of your values. For instance, the need for authenticity could also be a value that you want to embody in your daily life. Perhaps there will be times when you are caught in a frustrating interaction with someone, feeling the familiar pull to engage in behaviors that take you away from being authentic. When you can catch this happening, you can bring yourself back toward your authenticity, which puts you back on the path toward your values.

Steven C. Hayes, founder of Acceptance and Commitment Therapy, describes in his book *A Liberated Mind: How to Pivot Toward What Matters* that the more we try to avoid pain, the more likely we are to create more pain. Many of the cultural messages we've seen over the past few decades have centered on the premise that you shouldn't think negatively or experience negative emotions. The problem with this narrative is that it leaves many of its followers exhausted, frustrated, and lost.

You can't get rid of negativity in your life, but you can learn to live with it and make its role in your life less prominent. Whether we're dealing with a narcissistic mother who drains us, anxious thoughts that leave us stuck in rumination, or feelings of self-doubt looming over our head, negativity has a way of finding all of us. Central to Hayes's approach is the notion of psychological flexibility, which he defines as "the ability to feel and think with openness, to attend voluntarily to your experience of the present moment, and to move your life in directions that are important to you."[64] This is where our values come into play.

Hayes describes values as "chosen qualities of being and doing, such as being a caring parent, being a dependable friend, being socially aware, or being loyal, honest, and courageous. Living in accordance with our values is never finished; it is a lifelong journey."[65] Another quality Hayes suggests is that of taking committed action toward living in accordance with our values, which does not mean doing this perfectly or never straying from our values. Rather, it's a practice that we return to again and again.

We don't need to be perfectionists about our values, as that leads to psychological rigidity; rather it's about learning to course correct toward our values when we realize that we've gone off course. Equally important is the practice of showing ourselves plenty of grace when we aren't living by our values and reminding ourselves that this is what being human is all about. Making mistakes, course correcting, failing again only to learn a new lesson; this is what allows us to grow. Let's say you have a value of being present and one day you find yourself being anything but. Perhaps you're getting caught up in your thoughts where you end up ruminating, not being present in what you're doing. When you notice this happening, you can recognize "right, I'm getting caught in my thoughts," or "ah, autopilot. Take a second to breathe," and this puts you back in touch with your value of being present. The choice to move toward our values is there for us to make any time. You won't always get it right, and there will certainly be days when you will totally forget about your values. The point, however, is to accept this as part of life and know that your values don't go anywhere. They will always be available for you to return to.

64. Steven C. Hayes, *A Liberated Mind: How to Pivot Toward What Matters* (New York: Avery, 2019), 5.
65. Hayes, 22.

Chapter 5

ACKNOWLEDGING YOUR EMOTIONS AS A PATHWAY TO HEALING

Adult daughters of narcissistic mothers learned as children how to accommodate their mothers out of a survival necessity. Learning how to camouflage themselves, daughters become something of shape shifters. As a child, so much of who you are was driven underground, where not even you could find it. When you grew into your adult self, these self-hiding adaptations didn't just evaporate, they hung around like ghosts, ready to keep your core-self obscured. It takes significant work to excavate the underlying feelings that were buried in early childhood and to allow yourself the freedom to feel them in a *new context*. You are no longer that helpless young child who had to deny her real self in order to be what her mother needed her to be. You are an adult woman with a lot of years and wisdom under your belt. If you wish, you can go toward all of your feelings and begin to let yourself experience them in your body.

Alice Miller, trauma expert and author writes, "In analysis, the small and lonely child that is hidden behind his achievements wakes up and asks: 'what would have happened if I had appeared before you, bad, ugly, angry, jealous, lazy, dirty, smelly? Where would your love have been then? And I was all these things as well. Does this mean that it was not really me whom you loved, but only what I pretended to be? The well-behaved, reliable, empathic, understanding, and convenient child, who in fact was never a child at all? What becomes of my childhood? Have I not been cheated out of it? I can never return to it. I can never make up for it. From the beginning I have been a little adult. My abilities—were they simply misused?'"[66]

You may have heard before from either your own mother or simply the culture at large, that it does not do to dwell on your feelings. I'd like to make an addendum to this semi-true, semi-false statement. The truth is that *dwelling*, or the act of keeping feelings stuck in *thoughts*, rather than experienced in the body, will not lead to relief. Feelings are physical manifestations that show up in our body, and each emotion comes with its own impulse or motoric activations. For instance, rage will likely feel like heat in the belly and energy running down the arms and legs. Fists may even appear, and the impulse to kick, punch, or bite will be present. This doesn't mean you must act on these impulses; rather, it's about acknowledging their existence, which helps you stay fully connected to yourself.

Grief will likely emanate deep from within the belly, coming straight up through the throat, creating tears and sobs. The impulse with grief would be to cry, drop to the floor, and howl, and may even be commingled with rage, depending on the severity of the hurt. Joy may present physically as the impulse to hug, jump, smile, and laugh. You'll likely feel lightness all throughout your body. When feelings get cut off from the body and redirected into our thoughts, we don't get an opportunity to experience them physically, and therefore cannot attend to them in a way that would lead to release. Feelings that get stuck in thoughts will often lead to rumination and no action. When we are connected to our feelings, we are better equipped to adaptively take action in a way that best serves us. By action I don't mean *acting out* feelings destructively or lashing out; I'm referring to making an informed decision to use our feelings effectively.

For instance, Mary would often dwell on the thought that her mother was never going to change, causing her to experience significant depressive-like grief that would not relieve itself, and anger that would get caught in a spin cycle. When she was particularly angry with her mom for yet another boundary violation, she would say, "Why doesn't my mom understand?! I can't believe she would say all of those hurtful things to me." Of course, there is nothing wrong with expressing these thoughts, but Mary would chronically find herself bypassing her feelings in favor of getting stuck in her thoughts.

Her natural feeling of anger was trying to inform her of a boundary she needed to set with her mother, but her thoughts took over and she began to intellectualize. When we can get out of our thoughts and into our feelings, we are more likely to recognize what actions need to be taken. Intellectualizing keeps us hovering above our feelings where we're less likely to

---

66. Alice Miller, *Prisoners of Childhood: The Drama of the Gifted Child and the Search for the True Self* (New York: Basic Books, 1981), 15.

know what we need. When we're connected to our feelings, we have more choices and can actively use them to fulfill their wired-in purpose: to make changes, get closer to someone, create distance, find safety, etc.

When I talk about feelings, I'm primarily talking about the seven core emotions that can be identified as "fear, anger, sadness, disgust, excitement, joy, and sexual excitement."[67] These core emotions are neurobiologically wired within all mammalian brain systems.[68] We'll dive more deeply into some of the core emotions and what they mean later on. In our culture, we tend to speak in "I feel" statements, but rarely are we actually talking about emotions in their purest sense. There's nothing wrong with speaking this way, but for the purpose of this book, I'd like to encourage you to practice saying, "I feel" in reference to your actual feelings: anger, sadness, fear, lust/sexual excitement, care/love, joy, disgust.

You might find yourself saying things like, "I feel like he shouldn't have done that," or "I feel that her actions were wrong." These statements aren't inherently problematic, but again they may unintentionally obscure your connection to your real feelings because they are only describing your *perceptions* of events, rather than your *feelings* of events. What may be helpful in the above examples is to replace "I feel" with "I thought," "I believe," or "I sense," which would be more accurate. "I thought he shouldn't have done that," or "I believe that her actions were wrong." Practice using "I feel" only when describing emotions. In the next case example, you'll see this all come together.

Tara

"What do you mean, how do I feel toward her?" Tara asked with genuine confusion. I had just asked her, "What do you feel toward your mom when she rejects and ignores you like that? What feelings do you have toward her?" She had just listed off a litany of non-feelings, none of which were answering the question, and I sensed her frustration. "I feel that she was being so mean," she said. "And what do you feel toward her for being so mean?" I wondered. "Well, I think she's just such a nightmare to be around," Tara responded, and then followed up, "but I guess that's not really a feeling, is it?" Tara wasn't doing therapy wrong, nor did I have a particular answer I wanted from her. Rather, I was curious about her emotions, but she was telling me what she thought about her mother, not how she felt toward her. This was not her fault, as she had been raised to sublimate her emotions into her intellect, where feelings cannot be

---

67. Hilary Jacobs Hendel, *It's Not Always Depression: Working the Change Triangle to Listen to the Body, Discover Core Emotions, and Connect to Your Authentic Self* (New York: Penguin Random House, 2018), 136.

68. Jaak Panksepp, "Cross-Species Affective Neuroscience Decoding of the Primal Affective Experiences of Humans and Related Animals," *PLoS ONE*, 6, no. 9 (2011): e21236, https://doi.org/10.1371/journal.pone.0021236.

felt. I sat across her with sincere compassion for the way in which she had habitually been so disconnected from herself. "Um, I guess I feel...I feel...confused," she finally conceded and said, "What is the feeling I'm supposed to be having?"

Conversations like these occur regularly in therapy, particularly with adult daughters of narcissists, who have been taught to compartmentalize and suppress their natural feelings, urges, and impulses in favor of tending to the needs of others, namely their narcissistic parent. Narcissists often respond to their children's burgeoning emotions with disdain, contempt, ignorance, mocking, blankness, ridicule, gaslighting, and flat-out denial, especially if their child's feeling threatens them. Since narcissists operate from a very flimsy sense of self, largely fabricated by an ideal image that feeds off of others to sustain itself, they don't actually know what they feel, either. When a mother, who was emotionally stunted at a very young age and who was herself likely raised by narcissistic parents, attempts to raise a child, you essentially get two children trying to figure out their feelings. Children who are given proper emotional attunement and mirroring from their parents learn how to label their feelings and form a relationship to them.

Healthy parents will respond to their child's tears with care and interest, usually asking, "What's wrong? Are you sad?" The child will solemnly nod their head and the parent will say, "Tell me about what's making you sad, sweetie. It's okay to cry." This kind of attunement and mirroring helps children internalize a healthy relationship to their emotions so that when they grow up, they know how to regulate themselves with relative ease. Often, people mistakenly think that "healthy" or "normal" people don't experience emotional upsets, and will spend years in therapy attempting to get to the place where they, too, don't have painful emotions. What they may not realize is that healthy individuals know how to *relate* to their emotions and have learned ways to utilize their emotions adaptively. You, too, have this capacity and can strengthen your ability to tune into it.

Adult children of narcissists who were not emotionally attuned to can eventually get there through the support of a therapist who can help make this connection. I remember my own experience of realizing that I didn't need to fight against my emotions, but that I could show them curiosity and respect. It occurred to me that my feelings were going to exist within me for the rest of my life, so instead of wasting vital energy trying to control them, I could learn to have a relationship with them. Our feelings matter. Every emotion we experience has a wired-in purpose and reason for being. Similar to an ecosystem in which all parts are needed in order for it to thrive and function, every emotion is necessary to keep our own internal ecosystem working. There is no such thing as an emotion that doesn't belong.

A narcissistic mother will see her daughter's emotions as threats to her and will attempt to modify them to fit within her own narrative. Your mother will have no compunction about using your feelings against you. When you're rightfully angry over an injustice of some kind, she will tell you to stop making such a big deal. Your joy will shake up her foundation and to keep the scales even, she will find a way to burst your bubble. Tara's mother used to ridicule her when she would feel happy or accomplished, saying things like, "Why are you smiling? You're so ugly, no one who looks like you should have anything to feel happy about." When Tara protested in anger, her mom just laughed and walked away–a typical exchange that eventually led to Tara shutting down completely and entering a depressive state that would last for more than 20 years.

Unable to give voice to her emotions, Tara felt utterly lifeless, an effect of long-standing depression. Our work became about helping her notice, name, and respond to her emotions that lay dormant underneath her depressive affect. In some respects, the work Tara and I did was akin to helping someone who was severely paralyzed learn to walk again. This woman who had fought so hard to simply live her life was now learning how to sense something within her that most of us take for granted. Emotions have a purpose. Without them, we are lost.

Fortunately for Tara, her willingness to take this courageous step into the unknown, along with her fierce determination to reclaim what was stolen from her, allowed her depressive fog to lift and she could finally see what was alive in her. A major breakthrough for her was when she realized that her feelings did not threaten or disgust me; that they would not cause me to abandon or reject her, no matter what feeling she shared. Through our relationship, she eventually could label each and every emotion and its more nuanced forms, welcoming these lost parts of herself back into a relationship to her. I now asked Tara, "What do you feel toward your mom for the ways in which she treated you?" and Tara, without hesitation said, "I feel fucking angry. And sad for my little self. My anger feels like a white-hot fire that burns deep inside my stomach and when I really feel it, I notice myself releasing a bit of that judgment I held against myself for so many years. It's finally being felt toward *her* and not getting sucked back up where it would fester within me. Since I couldn't express my anger to her, I used to turn it against myself and say all of these mean things. All the horrible things my mom would say about me, I would start saying about me. The sadness comes in and tells me that I didn't deserve that kind of treatment, and that it was wrong to mistreat such a small child. I want to hold that little girl with tenderness." After three years of working so hard, Tara had finally broken through to the terrain of her emotions, these incredible forces that beckoned her home, and she was freer for it.

What is an emotion? Founder and director of the Yale Center for Emotional Intelligence, Marc Brackett, PhD, states in his book *Permission to Feel: Unlocking the Power of Emotions to Help Our Kids, Ourselves, and Our Society Thrive*, "feelings are a form of information. They're like news reports from inside our psyches, sending messages about what's going on inside the unique person that is each of us in response to whatever internal or external events we're experiencing."[69] Jaak Panksepp, acclaimed affective neuroscientist, claims that emotions are hardwired survival instincts that exist within all mammalian brain systems.[70]

Panksepp studied the brains of other mammals and found that "emotional circuits"[71] exist within the brain and can be categorized as such: SEEKING, ANGER, FEAR, PANIC/GRIEF, CARE, LUST, and PLAY.[72] What this means is that you are meant to feel! Your emotions are as integral and important as all other parts of your mind and body. Your vital organs keep you alive, your senses help you navigate your surroundings, and your nervous system alerts you to safety or danger. Your emotions are no different. They are hardwired for a reason.

When we spend our energy on trying to get away from what we feel, we inevitably create more pain and suffering for ourselves. The feeling that is needing attention gets ignored, and the information coming from it cannot be utilized. What usually happens when our feelings get ignored is that we then must rely on our defense mechanisms, such as numbing out through Insta-scrolling, getting stuck in our heads through rumination, avoidance, using something addictive to escape, or getting into an argument. None of these serve us in the end; they only work to temporarily get us disconnected from ourselves.

I'd like to come back to something we addressed earlier and differentiate between perceptions (or thoughts) and emotions. An emotion can be described using one word: anger, sadness/grief, joy, disgust, etc. Emotions exist on a spectrum and there are different shades to each one. However, for the time being, let's simply practice getting used to labeling our emotions according to their most basic forms. Even if anger feels more like annoyance, it still stems from anger in the end. Nervousness is a form of fear. How is that landing for you? Are you having any reactions to this? Just notice what comes up. We'll talk more about the body's role in expressing and feeling emotions later in the chapter.

---

69. Marc Brackett. *Permission to Feel: Unlocking the Power of Emotions to Help Our Kids, Ourselves, and Our Society Thrive* (New York: Celadon Books, 2019).

70. Karin Luisa Badt. "A Dialogue with Neuroscientist Jaak Panksepp on the SEEKING System: Breaking the Divide between Emotion and Cognition in Film Studies," *Projections* 9, no. 1 (2015): 66–79, https://doi.org/10.3167/proj.2015.090105.

71. Jaak Panksepp, "Cross-Species Affective Neuroscience Decoding of the Primal Affective Experiences of Humans and Related Animals," e21236.

72. Jaak Panksepp, "Cross-Species Primal Affective Experiences," e21236.

Perceptions are found within the mental story of the mind. When we're describing our perceptions of someone, we're usually assigning an intention, behavior, or belief to make sense of their action(s). Perceptions can be argued whereas feelings cannot.[73] For example, when I asked Tara what she felt toward her mom, she gave me a description *about* her mom rather than an emotion. "I feel she is a nightmare to be around" is a perception; "I feel anger toward her" is an emotion. We're in perception territory when "I feel" or "I felt" is followed by *that* or *like*. "I felt that it was irresponsible of her" is a perception.

When we're in emotions territory, our "I feel" statements are immediately followed by the feeling. "I felt disgusted by her actions" is a feeling. To help you communicate to yourself in a clearer way about what you're feeling, keep asking yourself, "How do I feel toward her for X?" Here's an imagined conversation, using some of Tara's statements to help lead us toward emotions.

> **Daughter:** My mom yelled at me the other day for wearing the wrong shirt. She said I looked stupid and unattractive.
>
> **Therapist:** Wow, that's awful! How did you feel toward her for saying that?
>
> **Daughter:** I felt that she was being unreasonable.
>
> **Therapist:** She was. What do you feel toward her for being unreasonable?
>
> **Daughter:** I feel that she shouldn't have done that.
>
> **Therapist:** And what do you feel toward her for doing that?
>
> **Daughter:** I guess I just felt betrayed.
>
> **Therapist:** And how do you feel toward her for betraying you?
>
> **Daughter:** I feel myself wanting to pull away.
>
> **Therapist:** If you didn't pull away, what would you be feeling toward her instead?
>
> **Daughter:** I would feel anger! I feel anger toward her.

As you can see in this exchange, no feeling was offered until the very end. You might look at that second to last exchange thinking, "But, feeling betrayed is a feeling!" Betrayed is not a core emotion; it is a description about the other person. They betrayed you. Emotions do live on a spectrum, and I do wish to convey that it is totally acceptable to offer other ways of expressing our feelings within their spectrum, such as annoyed, irritated, or aggravated. The reason I am belaboring the point of identifying your core emotions rather than using more descriptive terms like *annoyance* or *downtrodden,* for instance, is to help you have a new kind of foundation where your primary feelings are crystal clear to you.

---

73 Gabor Maté, "Compassionate Inquiry" (Training Course), 2019.

When I know exactly what core emotion I'm experiencing, I have a much clearer sense of what that means for me and how I want to show up in my relationships. In the past if I was feeling sad and someone asked "How are you feeling?" I would have said something like "Oh I'm just having a kind of blah day." While most of us understand the gist of "blah," it still reinforces a practice of keeping feelings vague. "Blah" is not a clear definition of anything. In fact, it's vague as hell! However, responding with "I'm feeling sad today," even though it may seem a strange thing to say (since culturally we are conditioned to keep those "bad" feelings under wraps), it allows for the emotion to be expressed clearly.

Once you are familiar with your core emotions and can identify them when they arise, then you might practice getting familiar with their more nuanced versions.

Emotions live on a spectrum, so it's inevitable that you will experience different degrees of them depending on the context. In the book *Permission to Feel,* Brackett shares that there are more words in the English language to describe our "negative" emotions than there are to describe the ones we consider positive, likely due to the fact that we tend to notice our unpleasant states more than our positive ones.[74] For now, however, let's simply start by getting comfortable using core emotion language to describe our emotions. This will help you reaffirm your connection to these basic, hardwired emotions that exist within all of us.

What did your mother teach you about your expressing your emotions?

Were your feelings met with interest, care, and patience, or were they mocked and denied? The way your mother related to your feelings will directly impact how you relate to them. If feelings like anger or sadness were routinely minimized or ignored, it's likely you will feel anxiety when these core emotions show up. The reason? Your nervous system has learned to equate feelings with punishment, or worse, flat-out intolerance, so it has adapted by sending you signals of distress when certain emotions arise. It's important to remember that you are working to override powerful forces that believe your feelings are dangerous, so don't get discouraged if you feel stuck.

When we cannot tolerate or know what we feel, we then have to rely on defense mechanisms that, after a certain point, become less and less effective. The purpose of this chapter is to help acquaint you with your emotions so that you can learn their language, glean the information that comes with them, and use them adaptively in your life. Great freedom comes when we know and care about what we feel. Symptoms like anxiety, depression, avoidance,

---

74. Brackett, *Permission to Feel,* 107–108.

withdrawal, or shame and guilt, which cause great suffering, can be lessened once you start to make friends with your feelings.[75]

Knowing what we feel is our birthright. When children are deprived of emotional attunement, they grow up with a deficit that leaves them unable to emotionally regulate or understand what their emotions are telling them. This is a huge loss to their emotional development. However, this needn't be a life sentence, as human beings are capable of making great change. One study exploring what leads to change in psychotherapy found that "patients' symptoms abate as they learn to identify, experience, and tolerate adaptive emotions that were previously suppressed, ignored, or dissociated. When our feelings can be felt, we become less symptomatic."[76] The study also found that "patients that enter psychotherapy in a state of emotional dysregulation are likely to have experienced early attachment relationships wherein their emotions were met with humiliation or rejection, rather than understanding, acceptance and coregulation. They have internalized these early attachment experiences as emotionally regulating internal working models that are expressed in adult attachment relationships."[77]

What reactions do you have about forming a relationship to your emotions? What comes up for you when you consider that all of your emotions are here to serve you? Notice if you start to feel any anxiety or uncertainty. Anxiety, while not considered a core emotion per se, is still an internal signal that is alerting us to a perceived sense of danger. Having anxiety over an emotion is a hallmark of being raised by a narcissist.

If you're feeling anxiety about the prospect of having permission to feel your feelings, let's consider: what is so dangerous about this? What dangerous things do you imagine could happen if you allow yourself to feel?

Most often, the biggest concern I hear is "I'll lose control," or "I'll drown in my emotions." The first statement is typically indicative of witnessing a family member lose control or fly off the handle. I wonder who that could be? Narcissistic rage is a very real phenomenon that is the result of a person who is *disconnected* from themselves, leading to an explosion. Typically, in a narcissistic rage, the individual is caught in a whirlpool of vulnerability, humiliation, and shame, which leads to a desire to retaliate by subjugating the other to humiliation or punishment. Many adult daughters fear that if they even touch on their anger, it will lead to an explosion much like the ones their mothers displayed. However, I

---

75. Rayna D. Markin, Kevin S. McCarthy, Amy Fuhrman, Danny Yeung, and Kari A. Gleiser, "The Process of Change in Accelerated Experiential Dynamic Psychotherapy (AEDP): A Case Study Analysis," *Journal of Psychotherapy Integration* 28, no. 2 (2018): 213-232, https://doi.org/10.1037/int0000084.

76. Markin et al., "Process of Change," 214.

77. Markin et al, 215.

would argue that we don't get to that kind of rage unless we are completely oblivious to the emotions building up inside, or in contrast, when we are actively trying to suppress our emotions.

As an example, I'll use ravenous hunger as the equivalent to rage. Have you ever gone several hours between meals because you were stuck at work or preoccupied with something, only to discover that you were *starving*? What happens when you realize you're starving? More than likely, you'll find yourself eating in abundance until your sense of being famished is annihilated. Let's rewind the tape and see what happens when hunger gets actively ignored. You're stuck at work, focusing on a document and you notice your stomach rumbling. Because you have to get this thing completed, you ignore it and grab a coffee. Thirty minutes go by and suddenly you get that pang again, only this time you're right at the wire and need to submit this document so that you can get home before it gets too dark out. You submit the document and on the drive home you notice feeling lightheaded and irritated by every single driver on the road.

By the time you arrive home, you feel like a walking skeleton in dire need of nourishment, so you frantically open all the cupboards, grabbing handfuls of crackers, bites of whatever you can find, while your dinner is being made. Had you responded to the fact that your body was calling out for food four hours ago, you would have avoided this frantic attempt to feed yourself. How does this relate to rage? A narcissist is not likely to notice her initial feelings of anger or irritation and respond to those states with much insight or self-awareness. You'll never hear a narcissist say, "Oh, I'm noticing some irritation right now. I think that means I need some space. Could you give me 30 minutes to just cool off?" She will hoard her irritated, angry feelings for later, for what she will deem as a justifiable explosion toward you or anyone who triggered her in the first place.

The blind rage (blind because of a disconnection from self), just like ravenous hunger, is the result of chronically ignoring or denying important internal signals that are attempting to get our attention. Signals like irritation, boredom, annoyance, frustration, and anger are all letting you know that something either needs to stop or change. The feelings and whatever is causing those feelings must be attended to.

Have you witnessed your mom fly into a blind rage? If so, what was your response to witnessing her explosive rage? What promise did you make to yourself as a result?

Many of the daughters I work with will tell me that they promised themselves they'd never allow themselves to get angry—an almost devout commitment to keeping their anger under wraps.

We often confuse having an emotion with *acting it out*. These are very different things. When I talk about emotions and helping yourself feel them, I'm talking about giving yourself the freedom and permission to have a relationship to yourself. You do this by having a desire to pay attention to what's happening in your body so that you can respond to those states with care. Responding to our emotions is not the same as acting them out. Tara Brach describes it like this: "You are in a state of presence (above the line) when you're aware of the blaming thoughts and physical experience of anger. During these moments, in addition to the anger, there's a sense of witnessing the anger and some choice in how you respond."[78] When we have an understanding of what our feelings are telling us, while staying connected to our values, we have more choices available to us for how we want to respond.

One study on affect regulation in children shows that children who have internalized their parents' responses, regulation, and attunement to their emotions will fare better in regulating their own emotions as they grow into adults.[79] Children who were in families where emotions were used as weapons against one another or swept under the rug are more likely to feel conflicted about how to respond to their own (or others') emotions as adults.

How this all comes together: When we are able to observe our emotional states, we are far less likely to act them out destructively. When you can register what you feel, your body will automatically relax and your prefrontal cortex (the front part of the brain responsible for decision making) will be more responsive. This will naturally create the space for you to be fully aware of your actions and choices.

The Core Emotions of Anger, Sadness, and Fear

I like to consider emotions as allies. They are here to help you make better decisions and connect more fully in your relationships. Depending on the situation, your feelings are also here to protect you. They each have a unique purpose, and when you can begin to see them as highly intelligent forces that are here to serve you, then you needn't waste energy fighting them. Of course, it doesn't mean you will like every feeling that visits, as some feelings like grief are painful, but the point is to know your feelings and accept them as they are.

Below I am going to list out three of the core emotions that most people struggle with: anger, sadness, and fear, as well as what the purpose of each is. Pay attention to how the descriptions land for you. Notice what reactions you have and jot them down on the blank

---

78. Tara Brach, *Radical Compassion: Learning to Love Yourself and Your World with the Practice of R.A.I.N.* (New York: Penguin Random House, 2019), 14.

79. Kathleen R. Delaney, "Following the Affect: Learning to Observe Emotional Regulation," *Journal of Child and Adolescent Psychiatric Nursing,* 19, no. 4 (2006): 175–181, https://doi.org/10.1111/j.1744-6171.2006.00069.x.

lines following each emotion or in a journal. Some questions to consider while reading these descriptions:

- Does this make sense to me?
- How was this emotion expressed or shown to me in my life?
- How did mom respond to these emotions when I expressed them to her?
- Were there other adults in my life that helped me identify and/or regulate these emotions?
- Do I want to have more freedom to feel this emotion in a healthy and adaptive way? If not, why? If yes, what do I hope more freedom to feel would offer me?
- If this feeling were a friend to me, what would it be telling me?

ANGER: This is probably the most difficult emotion for adult daughters to both experience and witness. Anger is considered to be a protest emotion. It will come up when you are witnessing or experiencing injustice, disrespect, or a loss of something important. Anger is a cue that lets us know that a boundary is being crossed, a valuable relationship is being infringed upon in some way, or an important aspect of our lives is being affected negatively (i.e., the grocery store closed before you had time to get food, or your quiet time is being disturbed by loud neighbors). Anger says, "I didn't like that."

Like any emotion, just because we feel something doesn't necessarily mean we *have* to do anything with it or express it. There will be times when expressing an emotion to someone may not be immediately available or the timing is off. However, take comfort in knowing that all emotions, when we feel them, notice them, and show them attention, can offer a world of relief.

Worded in another way, Dr. Brackett states that if we can feel our anger and make it useful, it will naturally start to abate. More specifically, he states that "if we can try to modify the injustice that sparked it, the anger will go away, because it's outlived its usefulness. If not, it will fester, even if it seems to subside.[80] Unfortunately, and not surprisingly, adult children of narcissists learn ways to sequester their emotions, particularly anger, to a less visible part of their awareness, where it festers.

Feelings that fester lead to so much damage. We may think we're "over it," but our anger remains, only this time it's no longer in our awareness. We don't want our emotions piling up like luggage on a baggage carousel, as this will lead to feeling overwhelmed. Our feelings like to be registered. They relax when they're seen by our observing mind, and we have

---

80. Brackett, *Permission to Feel,* 18.

a chance to live and respond with more vitality. Much like scratching an itch, once you've located and scratched it, the sensation of itchiness is gone. Feelings are no different. They are simply here to help us direct our attention toward an action or response that may lead to resolution.

Anger is very much like an inner protector. It pipes up when someone crosses a boundary or we feel unheard by someone close to us. Anger says, "Woah! Pump the breaks. Are you cool with this? I don't like what just happened. Can you protect yourself right now? Do you need to say something? Can you disengage with this person if they don't stop?"

When anger is less intense and is more a state of mild irritation or frustration, it's still alerting you to something valuable. Being frustrated may indicate that our attempts at getting something we want aren't working, so our desires end up frustrated. Irritation could be letting you know that you're starting to feel uncomfortable. I often communicate to my anger like this: "Yeah, I know that didn't feel good. I'm going to make sure I stand my ground and support myself. She may not have meant it in that way, but nevertheless I need to make sure my point gets heard."

Many daughters raised by narcissistic mothers have a hard time registering their feelings in general, however anger and sadness are among the hardest to connect with. Because narcissists fervently deny their own feelings of anger and sadness, they will do whatever it takes to evoke the same denial in their children.

Write down your reactions to this emotion and what you learned about expressing or showing anger.

BREAK FREE FROM NARCISSISTIC MOTHERS

SADNESS/GRIEF: Sadness or grief helps us move on from something devastating. When we are connected to our grief, much like the way a flowing river moves rocks and sediment, grief moves stuck energy through us so that we can move forward. Grief and sadness can often feel physically painful. Lodged in the throat, behind the eyes, and in the stomach, their physiological manifestations are usually the first to alert us to this feeling. When sadness gets stuck, you can practice by slowing your breath down and intentionally trying to open your throat by relaxing any tightening you feel. Imagine this sadness moving through you like a wave. It rises and releases, rises and releases.

Sadness or grief is saying, "Something or someone I value is gone, dying, changing."

Tears help us release stress hormones! They actually serve a purpose and can be incredibly healing when we allow them to flow, trusting that they'll stop when their job has been completed. Crying and feeling sadness or grief will come with a certain amount of pain and discomfort. To release pain, we have to feel it. But feeling pain is very different from avoiding it, which leads to a different, more lifelong kind of pain: depression, chronic stress or illness, panic attacks, anxiety, insomnia, and the list goes on. When pain gets avoided, resolution cannot be had.

Typically, when we're sad or grieving we shed tears. However, if tears and crying don't come, that's okay. This is not a sign that you're doing sad wrong, merely a sign that either something is blocking access to this expression or the intensity of the feeling is not as deep. We can feel sad watching a documentary about some devastation in the world, and not necessarily be driven to tears. And yet you may find yourself watching a children's movie, suddenly stunned as you notice yourself tearing up by a simple line of dialogue.

Sadness can motivate us to make changes in our lifestyle. For instance, when I watch a documentary on climate change, the sadness that I feel for the planet motivates me to change my lifestyle so that I'm more aligned with my environmental values. Other times, a flood of tears may pour out of me when I'm faced with something truly devastating, such as the death of a loved one, adjusting to life-altering news, or hearing about yet another injustice in the world that does so much damage.

When sadness is permitted to flow and we feel its impact by allowing ourselves to mourn and cry, it can release completely. When sadness gets comingled with states of helplessness and powerlessness, it can turn into depression. We are never truly helpless, and in some cases, we are mourning the fact that we don't have the level of power we wish we had to change something. However, take note of where you actually do have power. Power and choice are often one and the same. There is power in choosing to shop at small businesses, recycling plastic, writing to your legislature, standing up for someone being victimized, putting our needs first after a lifetime of oppression, owning up to a mistake we made, voting, and so on.

To prevent helplessness and powerlessness from taking over, it's helpful to notice what the narrative is as we're grieving or feeling sadness. Is the thought "this is stupid, I shouldn't be crying?" Are you attempting to minimize, devalue, or disconnect from the feeling? Stop yourself, and bring your awareness back to your body, notice the feeling anyway, and remind yourself that censoring or minimizing the feeling will only prolong its presence. Can you let that narrative go right now? Can you step outside of the habit of needing to rationalize or intellectualize your feeling away?

Renowned emotion-focused researcher Karla McLaren, whose ideas have heavily influenced my work, suggests that sadness be seen as a facilitator for letting go.[81] When something isn't working for us, we naturally cling tighter to it, and this creates tension in the body. Sadness, when it is truly allowed to flow through us, releases this tension and leads to relaxation.[82]

Below is one of McLaren's exercises that simulates what having healthy sadness feels like. It's a brilliant practice that I believe can offer you a sense of safety and sweetness for processing this sacred emotion.

"Breathe in until you feel a bit of tension in your chest and rib cage, and hold your breath for a count of three. (Don't create too much tension. If you're uncomfortable, let some air out before you hold your breath.)

As you breathe out, let your body go limp, relax your chest and shoulders, and feel the tension leaving your body. Let your arms hang loosely, relax your body, and let go.

Breathe in again until you feel a slight tension, hold your breath for a count of three, and this time, sigh audibly as you exhale and relax your body. Repeat one more time, and sigh out loud as you exhale and let go. If you feel relaxed and a bit less tense, thank the emotion that helped you. Thank your sadness!

I intentionally evoked your sadness by creating something that didn't work or feel right – which is the tension you felt when you held your breath. And then, I intentionally had you perform the actions your sadness requires; the sadness-specific actions involve relaxing, releasing, and letting go. Simple."[83]

---

81. Karla McLaren, "Welcoming the Gifts of Sadness," accessed June 28, 2021. https://karlamclaren.com/welcoming-the-gifts-of-sadness.
82. McLaren, "Welcoming the Gifts of Sadness."
83. McLaren, "Welcoming the Gifts of Sadness."

Write down your reactions to this emotion and what you learned about expressing or showing sadness.

....

....

....

....

....

....

FEAR/ANXIETY: Fear is about something that's happening *now*. Fear orients us to danger or novelty, and helps us take action. You want to have access to fear when you're in an unfamiliar neighborhood at night, or if you're hiking a trail that's known for bear sightings.

I equate my fear to my cat's ears when he is sensing something threatening. They curve back and flatten down his skull, and usually his gaze is very fixed. Fear is like that; it narrows our attention to what we are sensing as danger or threat in our environment. When fear is adaptive as in the above situations, it guides our decisions and orients us to take action that would ensure our safety.

When fear becomes maladaptive (i.e., it's not in response to imminent danger), it's more akin to anxiety. Adaptive fear orients us to danger *now,* whereas anxiety (or maladaptive fear) orients us to a possible danger in a future scenario. Typically, this type of anxiety is centered on what *could* go wrong and seems to convey that we won't have choices available to us to course correct.

For instance, a common anxious train of thought is "What if I do (insert here), and I fail at it? What if it doesn't work out? What if I just make a fool out of myself? What if so and so gets angry with me?"

You'll notice that these anticipations offer only one perspective: that of failure in some capacity.

What these anxious thoughts don't provide is a holistic perspective that takes into consideration questions like the following:

- Who are the people whom you'd be "exposed to?" Are they really going to be rejecting monsters?

- Would you really have no recourse?

- Is there no other way this could pan out? What if you didn't fail, but merely stumbled and did okay?

- Can people who make mistakes or are silly or foolish still be seen as good enough? Would you be so quick to judge and exile someone else for making a mistake in the way you imagine yourself making?

- Is there evidence that supports this belief? Is there evidence contrary to this belief? Are you only considering one side of the story?

One thing to consider is that anxiety is very good at maximizing negative outcomes and minimizing positive or neutral ones. You'll find that when you're anxious, your mind is only scanning for threat. This isn't a bad thing in and of itself. Where it becomes problematic is when you're lacking an awareness of what's happening. When you are aware, you're in a better position to observe it as a psychological function of the mind, *not the objective truth*. Awareness might sound like: "Okay, I'm anxious, so it's important to recognize that my mind is going to do that *thing.*"

Anxiety can be regulated by orienting ourselves to our internal and external anchors of safety, whether by acknowledging ourselves (internal) or making contact with the people or places that feel safe (external). Bringing our attention to the physiological manifestations in our bodies can help us notice how the anxiety is manifesting. This tracking of anxiety within the body allows us to get out of rumination and into a place of noticing. Paying attention in this way is like saying to ourselves, "What I'm feeling is important and deserving of my attention," and is in and of itself regulating. An example of an external resource would be to intentionally name all the ways in which you are safe in this moment. Or, if that's difficult, to bring your attention to all five of your senses, going through each to describe what you can feel, taste, smell, hear, and see. This offers an opportunity to ground in the present moment and get out of the storyline that's going off in your head.

When my body is experiencing anxiety, I know it's time to stop what I'm doing and pay attention. My anxious body feels soothed when I take in deep breaths, scan my reality for how safe I am, invite more of a holistic perspective to my thoughts, and remind myself that anxiety always passes.

It's helpful to notice, track, and stay with the anxiety until it goes down to a more manageable level. When we go straight to avoidance, numbing, or tuning out, we lose a vital opportunity to stay connected to ourselves. This connection, while it may not extinguish the anxiety the way some numbing strategies do (Do they really though?), creates, over time, a safe place *inside* of us that can hold our experiences mindfully and regulate our anxiety in a healthy manner.

When, through mindful awareness, we allow our feelings to be felt and to move through our bodies, we often feel better. If you notice yourself feeling hopeless, deflated, or empty, this may be a sign that a defense against feeling is in operation.

Check this out by doing a curious mental scan: What story am I attaching to this experience? Sometimes the mental story can contain all-or-nothing cognitions, catastrophizing, or "emotional reasoning" (i.e., "I failed, therefore I'm a failure"). Or we might be viewing our feelings with a sense of shame, disgust, or annoyance that they're there to begin with. Without meaning to, we can move away from our feelings for a variety of reasons. Offer yourself a dose of self-compassion for this, take a break, and when you're ready, bring your focus back to the feeling.

Self-compassion for feeling overwhelmed, blocked, or unaware of your feelings can look like these responses:

- "I don't have to get this right."
- "There is no grade for me to get. I'm learning and this takes time."
- "Wow, I'm overwhelmed. It's okay for me to take a break and come back to this later."
- "It sucks to feel stuck! A lot of people experience this, and learning to be with my feelings is still new. There's no right or wrong way to do this."
- "I can be kind to myself even when I'm struggling."

Write down how fear and anxiety manifest in your life. Explore how you understand the difference between fear and anxiety.

Tara Brach has a particular method that works to restore the mind back to a gentle observing state in which mindful self-compassion reigns: RAIN.[84] Those of you familiar with her work will recognize this practice. RAIN stands for Recognize, Allow, Investigate, and Nurture. In this practice, you are actively turning your attention to what is happening inside your mind and body with interest, care, and curiosity. To *Recognize* is simple: What is happening right now in my body? What feelings am I experiencing? The next step is to *Allow*: Let these feelings be. Let them exist without trying to fix them or judging yourself for having them. To *Investigate* invites you to pay attention with interest to what you are believing about yourself, others, or your situation. Ask the part of you that you are noticing, "What do you need from me?" To *Nurture* means putting all of this together and offering a caring and compassionate response to yourself. I like the definition of nurture, which I'll include here: "care for and encourage the growth or development of."[85]

Essentially, this practice activates our conscious awareness and takes us out of a trance, which Brach defines as being in a state of disconnection and autopilot.[86] In trance, we are less connected to what is happening to us and more wrapped up in our mind's story. When we step into presence, we're more likely to take stock in the literal and metaphorical scenery around us by asking questions such as, what am I telling myself about this situation? Is it creating more or less suffering? What do I most need in this moment?

Being present to ourselves doesn't require us to don yoga clothes or sit lotus style. I often think of presence as a willingness to pause and notice right here, right now. In a sense, presence is showing yourself mercy. In the book *Dune* by Frank Herbert, one of the main characters offers a revelation on the concept of mercy, stating: "It occurred to her that mercy was the ability to stop, if only for a moment. There was no mercy where there could be no stopping."[87] To be present is to stop with the intention to offer ourselves mercy, and it actively disrupts us out of trance.

---

84 Brach, *Radical Compassion*, 6-7.

85. *Oxford English Dictionary,* 2nd ed. (Oxford: Oxford University Press, 2004), s.v. "Nurture."

86. Brach, *Radical Compassion*, 8-11

87. Frank Herbert, *Dune* (New York: Ace Publishing, 1990), 245.

BREAK FREE FROM NARCISSISTIC MOTHERS

Chapter 6

BOUNDARIES

No is the first word we learn. As toddlers, we begin exploring our worlds with a series of no's trailing behind us. "No" is a complete sentence. As we grow up, "no" starts to feel like a bad word, something we shouldn't be saying in polite conversation. We're taught, in a multitude of ways, that "nice girls" give of themselves and ask for nothing in return. In the nice girl paradigm, saying no threatens an oppressive system that profits off of keeping women small and accommodating. What might happen if women all over the world suddenly decided to say no more often? Would we tolerate inappropriate behavior or cut it off as soon as it begins? Would corporations be able to profit from our insecurities, which they themselves created? No.

Growing up with a narcissistic mother most definitely reinforced the belief that *no* is a dirty word. As a child and even into adulthood, you may find yourself leaning into the belief that it's better to just say yes, grit your teeth, and get whatever was asked of you over with. Can we change that? As part of being a healthy, sovereign self, it is going to be necessary that you know your boundaries and feel entitled to them. You are leaving behind a relic of an old belief system that does not serve you anymore as an adult woman. What would you like to replace it with? Toxic beliefs can be overridden with more expansive and liberating ones, which are more likely to lead you toward a fuller life.

What comes up inside for you as you consider having boundaries? Do you find that your chest opens up and you feel a sense of relief, or are you flooded by anxious thoughts and fears? For most adult daughters, it's the latter. Narcissists do not like boundaries because it is a reminder of the natural separation that exists between all human beings. You know this acutely. In narcissistic households, boundaries are routinely crossed, invalidated, and questioned by the narcissist, and if you attempt to assert yourself, you are met with opposition. In this bind, most daughters learn that their best course of action is to stifle their feelings and tolerate their narcissistic mothers. Some daughters fear the consequences of what will happen if they set boundaries, while others feel completely overwhelmed with where to even begin.

Boundaries are necessary functions of healthy human relationships. They help us to feel safe with others, get our needs met, and keep our sense of autonomy intact. A boundary means, "I am allowed to be a separate individual with needs that won't look like yours and preferences that may not conform to your standards." Our boundaries are our power source. Without them, we are at higher risk for being in dangerous situations and taken advantage of. Consider your boundaries to be as essential to your wellbeing as food and water are to survival.

Precursors to boundaries are our feelings themselves and what is happening inside of our bodies. When we're connected to ourselves by listening to the language of our body, we will know what feels good and what doesn't. Our body communicates to us in myriad ways. Noticing our physiological sensations of distress (racing heartbeat, heat rising in the abdomen) and emotional activation (anger, irritation, or fear arising) gives us an opportunity to translate those sensations into words and actions, which become our boundaries.

We tend to get hung up on the desire to set a boundary *without hurting anyone's feelings* and can get overly focused on the wording itself. While it can be good to verbalize our boundaries in an honorable way, it's more important to know what our boundaries are and to feel completely entitled to them. The desire to set boundaries without causing emotional harm to others is understandable and normal, especially when you're attempting to undo the habit of people-pleasing. It's important to consider that you may have an overinflated sense of what will cause emotional harm to others, which makes sense given narcissism's impact on you. What will be essential, however, is to truly embody the belief that other people's feelings are not your responsibility. This does not mean you should be reckless or harmful as you go about setting boundaries, but it does mean that you are allowed to be clear and assertive with others in a manner that is respectful to both of you. What a person feels about your boundary is up to them to address and acknowledge.

As you begin this process, I encourage you to start out by practicing boundaries in small, non-threatening situations, such as politely saying no to a solicitor on the street, cancelling a plan that you agreed to out of guilt, unfollowing accounts on social media that don't serve you, and creating boundaries for yourself at home, such as saying no to being on your phone before bed.

⟩⟨ REFLECTION

Consider for a moment what you learned about boundaries from your mom. In what ways are your early childhood beliefs showing up for you as an adult?

At this point in your life, you've retained a kind of muscle memory for what interpersonal relationships look like. The rules are easily defined: Other people get to have needs and feelings and you don't. Should you have a feeling, need, or boundary, it would be best to keep it to yourself. Let's explore the cost this has on you.

⟩⟨ REFLECTION

What is the price you pay for putting others' needs first and not being entitled to your boundaries?

How might your life improve if you could allow yourself to have boundaries with others? What would free up for you?

What happens when your feelings or needs get pushed aside? What are the short-term and long-term costs to this?

BREAK FREE FROM NARCISSISTIC MOTHERS

If you've struggled with setting boundaries out of fear, know that you're not alone. Narcissistic mothers will create a lot of confusion about what you are entitled to and what your rights are in general. Fortunately, with enough practice, you'll come to see that setting boundaries can be simple and natural. The fear once associated with securing appropriate boundaries may be replaced with a healthy entitlement that allows you more freedom to honor your needs.

To truly be free of the clutches that your narcissist mother has on you, it's imperative that you live and breathe the belief that you have a *right* to exist outside of her. You also have the right to all of your feelings without needing to justify them, the right to attend to your needs as you see fit, and the biggest right of all: *the right to say no*. Hence we are spending this chapter exploring how you can really embody this knowledge and begin saying no whenever you want.

Boundaries are essential components of healthy and consensual relationships. That means we must communicate them to the people in our lives in order for them to be effective. Since you are an adult and no longer dependent on your mother, it's important that you truly recognize how free this makes you. You may not feel free because on an energetic level you're still chained to her rules and standards. She may continue to find a way to cross the line, invalidate your feelings, and intrude upon your life without asking, awakening old dynamics that kept your feelings from being powerful. The kind of freedom I'm referring to is one that all adults possess whether they recognize it or not: the freedom to know oneself, one's limits, and one's choices. This is a revolution of "my boundaries, my choice," an offshoot of "my body, my choice."

As an adult woman, you get to set the pace of your interactions with your mom. You are no longer that child who had to put up with abusive behavior out of a survival necessity. In essence, you're taking your power back. Like any healthy rebellion, it starts with an awareness of injustice and a desire to disrupt power imbalances that lead to dis-ease. Standing up for yourself, saying no, and asserting your limits are acts of self-empowerment that ripple out into the culture. Your children, partners/spouses, friends, family, and colleagues will benefit from witnessing as you honor your boundaries. It's a loving act of defiance that instills hope, healing, and trust in self. Dr. Faith Harper, psychotherapist and author of *Unfuck Your Boundaries*, describes it this way: "Boundaries are about claiming your own space, not claiming other people's space."[88]

I'd like to offer some definitions that may be helpful to you as you begin exploring your boundaries. We'll break down physical and mental/emotional boundaries. You will likely discover other types of boundaries that exist for you outside of these two realms (and they

---

88. Faith G. Harper, *Unfuck Your Boundaries: Build Better Relationships through Consent, Communication, and Expressing Your Needs,* 2nd ed. (Portland: Microcosm Publishing, 2019), 7.

do exist). Welcome their inclusion. Dr. Harper shares a list of additional boundaries outside of these two: property boundaries, sexual boundaries (which I have lumped into physical boundaries), emotional-relational boundaries, intellectual boundaries, spiritual boundaries, and time boundaries.[89] You have the right to determine your boundaries, including deciding what they are and how they are enforced.

A physical boundary encompasses our physical body, the space we live in, and our personal bubble. Your clothes are a boundary protecting your body from being exposed to the environment. Your home is a physical boundary that protects you from harsh weather conditions and is ideally a safe haven from the wider world. Think of all the physical boundaries that surround you and how they offer you safety and protection.

I'd like to offer you some statements as reminders of the rights you have to your physical body.

I have the right to determine:

- Who is allowed to touch my body.
- How my body is touched and the right to opt out of unsafe touch or any touch I no longer want.
- How close someone gets to me in public, at home, at work, or with a group of people.
- Who enters my home (or any physical space I inhabit) and when.
- How and when I feed and care for my body.
- My sexual preferences, including how and when I engage physically and with whom; how and when I engage sexually and with whom.

An emotional and mental boundary defines what we allow in our emotional and mental space. We can identify an emotional and mental boundary by noticing how we feel about what is happening, what we will allow ourselves to be exposed to psychologically, and what information we choose to take in or leave out. As an act of both healthy rebellion and emotional wellbeing, I decided that a major emotional and mental boundary for me was limiting my news intake. I've determined that being bombarded with news media in any form, even the media that supports my beliefs, has a detrimental effect on my wellbeing. I don't mind others sharing with me about world events they're interested in, but I cannot tolerate listening to or reading the news in the way it is broadcast. At least for the time being. Another mental and emotional boundary is setting limits on aggressive and/or abusive

---

89. Harper, *Unfuck Your Boundaries,* 13–14.

BREAK FREE FROM NARCISSISTIC MOTHERS

verbal behavior. I will always accept people expressing their feelings, but I will set a firm boundary in the face of harmful, denigrating, or disrespectful words being hurled at me.

Let's explore your emotional and mental boundaries through affirming statements that remind you of your rights to them.

I have the right to determine:

- How much emotional labor I put into a conversation.
- If my feelings are being disregarded and devalued, and either leave the conversation or assert my rights.
- If I sense I am being gaslit, manipulated, or disrespected, I can end the conversation completely.
- What topics of conversation I am comfortable discussing with others.
- When I feel emotionally uncomfortable; and if I do, I have the right to set a limit.
- Whether I feel safe or unsafe sharing my emotions with someone.

Building healthy boundaries is not the same thing as putting up walls around you. When you are operating from within your boundaries, you are in a state of protection that allows you to maneuver in the world and in your relationships. You want your boundaries to give you the space to meet your own needs and have enough flexibility to meet the needs of others in a way that is mutually respectful. Boundaries do not have to be completely rigid, but there will be times when rigidity is essential.[90] Issues related to safety can be nonnegotiable—such as wearing a seatbelt, saying no to physical or sexual violations, keeping your door locked, safeguarding financial information, protecting your emotional wellbeing against verbal abuse, and anything else you deem essential to your safety.

Narcissists are threatened by boundaries. When you are connected to your boundaries, it becomes very difficult for narcissists to extract their supply of compliance from you. It is not uncommon for adult daughters to witness an increase in their mothers' hostility and rage when they begin to practice setting boundaries. As challenging as it is for anyone to set boundaries, adult daughters of narcissistic mothers will find this act to feel Herculean. However, like anything we put our effort and practice into, we'll get better at it.

There will be plenty of moments where self-doubt, guilt, and anxiety will step forward and instruct you to stand down. These are psychological functions from childhood and adolescence that inhibited you out of a need to keep your mother happy and you safe. Imagine a twelve-year-old being told by her mother that if she doesn't do what her mother tells her, she

---

90. Harper, *Unfuck Your Boundaries,* 16.

will be beaten, ridiculed, abandoned, humiliated, punished, or otherwise hurt. Or consider the perspective of a seven-year-old who asked for what she needed, only to witness her mother melt down into a helpless puddle where she informed her daughter that her needs were "too much to handle."

Guilt, self-doubt, and anxiety were there to pull you back and keep you safe from a mother who was either "too burdened" by you or far too frightening to provoke. Now you can create a different route for your needs to travel. But be mindful that old habits die hard. The guilt, self-doubt, and anxiety may attempt to pull you back into staying small when you start asserting your needs and boundaries. It's so important that you recognize these forces as old protectors that you don't need as an adult when it comes to communicating your boundaries with your mother. You have something else to protect you: you.

Some questions for you to consider:

- If I didn't doubt myself, how would I be showing up differently in this conversation?
- What am I most afraid of? How is what I fear a threat to me now?
- What is this guilt about? What "wrong" did I commit? Would I encourage anyone else to feel guilty about this? Am I attempting to take ownership of my mother's feelings?

Words aren't always required when setting a boundary. There will be times when you may need to place a physical distance between you and another person. Boundary setting can also be done for future events, such as letting a colleague know that next week, you're not going to be able to have lunch with them due to a deadline, or informing a spouse that in the future you would prefer they not invite their friends over without telling you first.

Notice what comes up for you when you read the following scenarios. Pay attention to any indication of feeling uncomfortable, irritated, fearful, or when you don't like something. Your emotions, body sensations, and needs will alert you to when you feel safe or unsafe, and I invite you to notice this as you read through these scenarios. I'll ask if you can set the boundary. In some cases, you may not need to, so pay attention to when you find that a boundary is not needed.

Remember: boundaries can be stated in words, through physical acts, and as requests regarding future events.

SITUATION 1

You're at a movie theater with a friend and someone unfamiliar sits next to you. Journal your reaction:

Can you set the boundary?

If setting the boundary was difficult, what held you back?

SITUATION 2

You are given a work promotion and all of your colleagues signed a card for you and bought you a gift certificate for a week's worth of coffee. Journal your reaction:

_____

_____

_____

_____

_____

Can you set the boundary?

_____

_____

_____

_____

If setting the boundary was difficult, what held you back?

_____

_____

_____

_____

SITUATION 3

Your mom calls you and immediately begins with a tirade on the latest news reports and gossip from her local community. She doesn't ask about how you're doing or what you're up to. Journal your reaction:

Can you set the boundary?

If setting the boundary was difficult, what held you back?

SITUATION 4

You're in a rush at the grocery store and a clerk strikes up a conversation with you that doesn't seem to be ending any time soon. Journal your reaction:

....

....

....

....

....

Can you set the boundary?

....

....

....

....

If setting the boundary was difficult, what held you back?

....

....

....

....

SITUATION 5

While giving you a massage, the masseuse uses too much pressure on your shoulders. Journal your reaction:

Can you set the boundary?

If setting the boundary was difficult, what held you back?

SITUATION 6

You're at a restaurant and your order gets messed up. You end up with a dish that you do not want. Journal your reaction:

....

....

....

....

....

Can you set the boundary?

....

....

....

....

If setting the boundary was difficult, what held you back?

....

....

....

....

The Why

It can be helpful for those with whom we set boundaries to know what we want, and in some cases, why we want those things. I emphasize *some* cases because there will be times when the why is not important. This all depends on the person and the way they are treating you. For instance, if you're needing to set a boundary with a coworker whom you get along with relatively well, you may say something like, "Hey Emma, would you mind turning your music down? It's a little distracting to me." In this instance, you're asking for what you want and providing the reason.

With individuals who you find hostile or disrespectful, a simple statement will suffice. Whoever fits this bill, your boundary statement may look like: "I don't want to have this conversation right now." If they ask, "why?" in a manner that invites defensiveness and intimidation, you can say, "Because I don't want to," or simply repeat, "I don't want to have this conversation right now."

Your mother may fall somewhere in between these two polarities. Don't worry about getting the wording right so much as getting the words out! Let's not make the goal about "perfect boundary setting" (because that's not a thing), and instead invite realness, which can sometimes be messy and clunky. Over time, your boundary setting techniques will become more refined and a lot easier to access.

To practice, I'm going to offer some boundary-setting statements I encourage you to try on individuals with whom you feel some measure of safety. Once you've practiced with these folks, putting your boundaries into practice with your mother will be the next step. If you don't have healthy people to practice these skills with, simply practice them in your head, out loud in a safe space, or with your therapist.

Boundary-setting statements:

- I prefer not to do that.
- No.
- No, thank you.
- I'm going to have to cancel tonight.
- Stop.
- Can you please give me some physical space?
- I'd like more time alone.
- I won't be doing that.
- This topic is off-limits for me.
- I'd like for us to talk about this later.
- I feel uncomfortable with that, so I'd like to pause.
- I need to take a break.
- I'm going to be unavailable this weekend.

- Not today, but how about next week?
- I have to leave by 10pm (or I'm leaving at 10pm).

Feel free to take the above and tweak them a bit to fit the way you might speak to a friend. Keep the boundary statement in there and make sure it's still clear. Next, we'll explore lengthier boundary setting statements that might feel more natural to you.

Lengthier statements:

- I don't want you coming over unannounced anymore. Can we work out a better system that's good for both of us?
- When you call me several times per day, I get distracted. I won't be answering your calls, but I'm willing to make a plan to connect during the weekend.
- I appreciate your wanting to give me advice, but I'm going to ask that you not. It's really important to me that I make this choice by myself.
- Can you let me know the next time you won't be available? That way I can plan around it better.
- I know you're stressed, but right now I don't have the emotional bandwidth to support you in the way you need. Can we talk about this tomorrow morning?

A simple boundary-setting "equation" that you can use has three components: I feel, I need, I'd like (or Would you be willing?).

Some examples include:

- I feel uncomfortable and I need some time to decompress. I'd like to resume this conversation tomorrow.
- I am feeling really overwhelmed and tired. I need some emotional connection. Would you be willing to hang out with me tonight over a glass of wine?
- When I feel outraged like this, I really need to vent my feelings in my journal. Would you be willing to call me back in an hour?

Veering from the Script

When we're setting boundaries, we don't have to be robotic or follow a script every time. We can use our empathy skills to help the other person understand where we're coming from and why our boundaries are important to us in that moment. There are times when I might tell someone I love, "Hey, I don't know why, but I'm really irritable today. Just a heads-up that I might need some space." Sometimes we won't always know where a boundary might be needed, however your emotions will alert you to when it's time to set one.

With narcissists, their worldview is tragically skewed to see people and situations as either all good or all bad. In psychoanalysis, this is called *splitting*. Dr. Joseph Burgo, psychoanalyst and author of *Why Do I Do That? Psychological Defense Mechanisms and the Hidden Ways They Shape Our Lives*, defines splitting as a mechanism whereby we take complex feelings (i.e., when you love someone but have strong feelings of anger toward them) and split them off into categories of either/or.[91] This psychological defense mechanism offers us a solution for ambiguity and mixed feelings.

Your mother has likely engaged in splitting most of her life, as this gave her a clean and simple way of categorizing people and herself. The "you're either with me or against me" dichotomy rules her emotional landscape. If you go against her wishes, identify your separateness, set a boundary, she will likely take that as an assault against her sense of self. When you are different from her, this will inevitably bring up her own mixed feelings toward you, which threaten her sense of continuity. To combat this, she will split you off as either all good or all bad, depending upon the feeling she's having.

Many adult daughters have found that in the past (or present), it was easier to cave, grit their teeth, and pacify their mother by complying to her wishes. Instances like staying on the phone for hours at a time despite wanting to run errands, or putting up with invasive behavior during holidays are common among daughters of narcissists. In these instances, they put up with the behavior in order to be the all-good daughter and perhaps even get the all-good mother in return. As adult women in recovery, however, they are having to contend with the fact that subjugating themselves to their mother's behavior only takes them backward, especially if it is done without boundaries. However, what can feel almost worse is taking steps toward enhancing their self-care and independence, as that gets registered as unacceptable transgressions against their mothers (usually by their mothers).

Consider your own mother's reactions as very misguided attempts at self-protection. Ultimately, her reactions are not about you, though you have been primed to think so. The more you can hold that in your mind, the less likely you are to take her reactions personally or relate to the all-good/all-bad daughter narrative as truth. Her verbal attacks against you, whether they are in person, over the phone, or through text, email, or letter, are her misguided attempts at self-protection. You no longer have to fall in line the way you've been trained to do in these instances.

---

91. Joseph Burgo, *Why Do I Do That?: Psychological Defense Mechanisms and the Hidden Ways They Shape Our Lives* (Chapel Hill, NC: New Rise Press, 2012), 83.

The healthiest thing you can do is learn to withstand the initial discomfort of setting your boundaries and recognize that any response that uses devaluation, fear mongering, gaslighting, manipulation, verbal abuse, or coercion is unreasonable, not your boundaries themselves. You do not have to accept or put up with abusive behavior as you embark on this practice. As you begin setting boundaries, know that you are engaging in positively disrupting a toxic dynamic for the betterment of your mental health and wellbeing. Consider yourself part of a large group of women around the world who are attempting to change the status quo with their narcissistic mothers and undo familial injustice.

❭❬ EXERCISE: SETTING BOUNDARIES

I'd like for you to consider your current boundaries with your mother and check off whether they are lacking, needing improvement, or right on track. Then write down how you might disrupt the toxic dynamic, set your boundaries, and better your mental health.

Do you feel you are entitled to tell your mother when she can call you or come over to your house?

        ❑ lacking   ❑ needs improvement   ❑ right on track

Are you able to interrupt her words when they become too much, critical, or abusive?

        ❑ lacking   ❑ needs improvement   ❑ right on track

Are you allowed to be angry toward your mother and express your needs that are not being fulfilled?

      ❏ lacking   ❏ needs improvement   ❏ right on track

Can you change plans with her freely or are you obligated to follow through?

      ❏ lacking   ❏ needs improvement   ❏ right on track

Do you feel you are entitled to what you feel or need when interacting with her?

      ❏ lacking   ❏ needs improvement   ❏ right on track

Do you feel you owe your mother a lengthy explanation of your needs, feelings, or boundaries in order for them to be valid or heard?

❏ lacking   ❏ needs improvement   ❏ right on track

When your mother disagrees with you or expresses anger, do you feel the need to take responsibility for her feelings by bowing down or minimizing what you feel or need?

❏ lacking   ❏ needs improvement   ❏ right on track

Do you feel you must go along with your mother's requests of you, even when you do not want to?

❏ lacking   ❏ needs improvement   ❏ right on track

Does saying no to your mother provoke disproportionate guilt, or do you feel entitled to your boundary?

❏ lacking ❏ needs improvement ❏ right on track

There will always be room for improvement when we assert our boundaries. Consider the above questions as insights into where you can practice engaging in more assertive behavior with your mother.

Self-Assertion

In the *Assertiveness Workbook: How to Express Your Ideas and Stand Up for Yourself at Work and in Relationships*, Randy Paterson offers a suggestion that you may find useful here. In his book, he highlights the importance of tracking your responses in a journal or worksheet format and checking out whether they fall into the category of passive, aggressive, assertive, or passive aggressive. Tracking responses like this allows us to take inventory of how our words landed and whether or not we expressed ourselves assertively.

I will include the guiding questions Paterson outlines in his workbook on page 5, changing some of the wording only slightly.

◗ EXERCISE: TRACKING RESPONSES

Go back to a recent situation with your mom. Describe what happened, including what she said or did, and identify how you responded:

Looking back on that, did your response articulate your feelings, needs, and boundaries with integrity and clarity, or was it clouded in passivity:

Were you aggressive toward her or passive aggressive?

How did the interaction turn out?

What did you feel afterward?

Can you identify an alternative response that clearly conveys what you feel in a more assertive way?

....

....

....

....

Focus on making smaller improvements in your communication style over time, rather than big sweeping changes in one go. Some of you may feel completely ready to do a massive overhaul in the way you communicate starting right now, while others may decide that making slow and steady changes is going to serve you better. Do what's right for you.

What are some examples of requests or demands that your mother makes of you? How would your life change if you were able to say no? What are the current beliefs that prevent you from being assertive and saying no or setting a boundary?

In the *Assertiveness Workbook*, Paterson outlines a few concepts for strengthening self-assertion that are worth sharing. With enough practice these will start to feel like second nature.

His first recommendation is "Don't apologize when it isn't necessary."[92] When we apologize for our needs or desires, we unconsciously transmit the message that "I'm in the wrong." There's nothing wrong with apologizing when we have to cancel plans or if we've hurt someone we care about, but when you begin a statement with "I'm sorry" for something that's not worth apologizing for (like setting a boundary), it cuts your confidence off at the root.

Paterson also recommends that you "don't defend yourself or make excuses when it isn't necessary."[93] When we offer excuses, we are implying that the reason we can't do something or be available is due to a barrier, which "invites the other person to help you find a way around the barrier."[94] If you try to offer your mother an excuse for why you are unable to

---

92. Randy J. Paterson, *The Assertiveness Workbook: How to Express Your Ideas and Stand Up to Yourself at Work and In Relationships* (Oakland: New Harbinger Publications, 2000), 152.
93. Paterson, *Assertiveness Workbook*, 152.
94. Paterson, *Assertiveness Workbook*, 152.

give her what she wants, she may use that as ammunition against you or see it as an opening to victimize herself. In all likelihood she'll do this anyway, but this is your practice to implement skills that will reinforce your right to say no without needing to make an excuse.

Another suggestion is "don't ask permission to say no,"[95] which is essential when you're starting out. "No" is often diluted when we ask if it's okay for us to have a basic right to what we need, and conveys the message that the other person is the gatekeeper to our boundaries. This unconsciously gives other people power over you, which will make setting your boundaries feel like you are not entitled to them.

The last two assertiveness positions Paterson recommends are "Don't wait for acceptance" and "Accept the consequences."[96] Both of these are reminders that not everyone is accepting of our boundaries and, in some cases, may feel threatened by your change in behavior. If we wait for acceptance, the practice of self-assertion gets stalled and we stay stuck.

When practicing assertiveness with your narcissistic mother, the consequences may include verbal abuse, stonewalling, inappropriate communication (texting you for hours), public humiliation, gossiping with friends, or guilt tripping. You should be prepared for her to dislike your newfound sense of self, and accept that you may need to distance from her to protect your wellbeing. In some cases, your mother may surprise you and be tolerant of your boundaries. Celebrate those moments!

As you do this work, it's important that along the way you either have or establish a strong support network, be firmly planted in recognizing your basic human rights, and practice being utterly kind to yourself. The emphasis here is all about honoring *you* by laying claim to your birthright to have healthy boundaries and permitting yourself to say no to what doesn't serve you. Changing your mom is out of the question, but you can change yourself and how you relate to her.

---

95. Paterson, *Assertiveness Workbook*, 152.
96. Paterson, *Assertiveness Workbook*, 153.

BREAK FREE FROM NARCISSISTIC MOTHERS

Chapter 7

TOXIC SHAME

Shame is a profoundly dysregulating, body-centered experience of unworthiness. Evolutionarily speaking, shame is an affective state that informs us when we've done something against our morals or value system, or have significantly gone against social norms. It is a social emotion geared toward regulating inappropriate behavior that may go against societal, cultural, or familial rules. When we're in a healthy state of shame, that is, capable of relating to it without *identifying* with it, we can utilize its pull to right our wrongs. When shame becomes *toxic* (a term introduced to me by Susan Warren Warshow, LCSW, LMFT), or rather, when we are consumed by it in such a way that it causes us to feel "all bad" without any redeeming qualities, it can generate feelings of hopelessness and a desire to hide away or become avoidant in relationship to others. This type of shame can get reinforced by narcissistic mothers who, because they cannot tolerate their own feelings of inadequacy, project it onto their children. These children eventually come to believe that they are fundamentally unlovable and deficient, and will be "found out" by those in their workplace, community, or intimate relationships. This being "found out" is replete with anxiety and a chronic sense that any misdeed or mistake will be an opening for others to ridicule and reject them.

Shame is also a relational emotion. It is insidious, etched in the face of a devaluing caregiver who looks at her child with contempt and disgust. Inevitably this experience becomes the beginning stage of never feeling "good enough." Because the experience of shame gets registered in our right hemisphere, the part of our brain that does not contain language or logic,[97] it becomes what psychotherapists refer to as a "felt sense." Consider for a moment a dog who is being scolded for knocking the garbage over and making a mess. Even if the owner is ridiculing him in a teasing way, the dog will look down, tremble, cower and become the full embodiment of shame. We all know exactly what the dog is feeling because his body is showing the markers of what "being a bad dog" (shame) looks like.

As you do this inner healing around your own experience of shame, I encourage you to work with a therapist who is trained in somatic and emotion-focused therapy. When our right hemisphere has an affective experience (an emotion), the left hemisphere, responsible for language and logic, begins to weave a story, using the language of our caregivers to regulate the experience.[98] For example, if your mother ridiculed you every time you felt sad and cried, she conveyed to you that your sadness was wrong and should remain hidden. Now as an adult, when something triggers sadness, you may notice an uptick in negative self-assessments ranging from "I'm weak for feeling this way" to noticing a force inside attempting to submerge your feelings out of your awareness.

What I'd like you to know in this moment is that your core shame, the "not good enough" experience, is based on a lie. Core shame, or the experience that one is inherently bad, fraudulent, or unworthy was taught to you by a severely psychologically impaired mother who also internalized significant shame as a child. Because she does not have the capacity to be attuned to you as a separate self, she will transmit that inability onto you in the form of shame. Her shame becomes your shame. This lie was perpetuated over and over again and does not bear the truth of who you are. There is a You experiencing the shame. You can't both experience shame and be the shame, just like you cannot watch a cloud and be the cloud at the same time. You are the watcher of the sky, just like you are the experiencer of shame, not *the* shame. So, who is the observer of this shame? If you are not the shame, but merely experiencing it, who is the You underneath?

97. Patricia A. DeYoung, *Understanding and Treating Chronic Shame: A Relational/Neurobiological Approach* (New York: Routledge, 2015), 37.

98. Patti Ashley, *Shame-Informed Therapy: Treatment Strategies to Overcome Core Shame and Reconstruct the Authentic Self* (Eau Claire, WI: PESI Publishing & Media, 2020), 23.

◗ REFLECTION

Take some time to reflect on this. If shame wasn't interfering with your sense of self, who would you be?

I'd like to remind anyone who is hooked by their shame and unable to imagine being anything other than what your shame is telling you, to recognize that this will be a new concept for you. The idea of relating to shame as an experience, rather than as a "truth" about you is difficult for many. You have likely been taught through a myriad of ways to see yourself as inseparable from the shame. Being routinely shamed in childhood or adolescence gets implanted in your right hemisphere, the part of your brain that holds abstract nonverbal concepts like emotions and memories. The left hemisphere, the part responsible for language, starts to write a story to support the distressing feeling of shame as a way of integrating the experience into one cohesive narrative. The problem is that, over time, the *story* of shame starts to feel true, akin to factual evidence.

With enough shaming experiences, you and the shame started to feel like one entity—no space between you and it. However, you were not born ashamed, you had to be taught *how to be* ashamed.[99] A common response to this can sound like "But it has to be true; my mother shamed me all the time. I know it's true. She wouldn't have done it if it weren't true." In such cases, I like to remind my clients that narcissists themselves have a great deal of

------

99. Bridget Quebodeaux, LMFT, in discussion with the author, 2020.

unconscious shame that they are constantly battling and have to find ways to split off from themselves. Donald Winnicott, a famous psychoanalyst from the 1950s, coined the term *false self* to define a defense unconsciously created by individuals who must deny their real feelings in order to comply with the demands of others.[100] Over time, the real feelings lying underneath threaten this false self and can lead to a great deal of shame.

Narcissism is the false self that covers up deeply entrenched shame. As you may know, shame is a disorienting and isolating emotion that spins a toxic narrative around who we think we are. Narcissists never learned how to relate to or understand their real feelings and eventually associated them with being a threat to their self-esteem. As a means of reducing the impact of their feelings, they had to deny them outright, relying exclusively on defense mechanisms. Because individuals with narcissism experience high degrees of shame, they have to put it somewhere outside of themselves. This leads them to rely on other people to absorb and take ownership of their own shame.

When we ignore, deny, or reject our feelings, they don't simply evaporate. Feelings have to go somewhere. Feelings that go unacknowledged become something else and will either get internalized, where they can become symptoms of anxiety and depression, or projected "out there" where the person no longer has to carry the feeling and instead relates to others as if *they* were the ones with the feeling. A narcissist will go to great lengths to preserve their self-image, even at the expense of their own child: you. You become the shame-container.

Your success, independence, feelings/desires, and anything that emanates from your real self will threaten your mother's sense of self. Since she relies on your smallness to stay psychologically balanced, anything that threatens this delicate equilibrium will trigger her need to overrule your reality with hers. If you surpass your mother in success, she will knock you down. If you get bullied at school, she will blame you as the cause. If you are overwhelmed with your day, she will have it worse. Are you seeing the pattern here?

Could you imagine ever telling your child, or any child for that matter, that they were the cause of your unhappiness or deserved abuse from others? That they were unworthy of love because they hurt your feelings or didn't clean their room? If you answer no, then I hope you can register the insanity of a shaming mother. No child should ever be shamed, bullied, or abused for who they are or for what they feel or need. Yet sadly this happens over and over again in narcissistic households. Shame becomes the hooded figure lurking around every corner, waiting to demolish anyone in its path. This is why I'm suggesting that you consider the shame you took in as a lie. It was never about you being unworthy, it was about an impaired mother unable to offer you the type of relationship that every child

---

100. Robert Ehrlich, "Winnicott's Idea of The False Self: Theory as Autobiography," *Journal of the American Psychoanalytic Association*, 69, no. 1 (2021): 75–108, https://doi.org/10.1177/00030651211001461.

BREAK FREE FROM NARCISSISTIC MOTHERS

needs. Children should never have to earn a caring relationship with their mother. It is their birthright to be protected emotionally and physically.

Let's go back in time for a moment. Can you recall an image of yourself as a young girl? Maybe she was just shamed for something innocuous or made to feel insignificant for displaying a totally normal feeling or need. Imagine what she's feeling right now. What is she needing from a caring adult that she's not getting? Can you take a moment to help her? I invite you to extend warmth and empathy toward her, offer her a space to feel her feelings, and hold her with real tenderness. You are also welcome to stand up to your mother here too. Invite your adult self to shield your small self and set a limit with your mom. Tell her that she cannot speak to you in that way. Make the boundary explicitly clear.

Patti Ashley, shame-informed therapist, describes how children internalize beliefs, stating, "Children observe and download a caregiver's beliefs as their own."[101] Children cannot perceive the world like adults do[102] and do not have the capacity to recognize that their mothers are impaired. Quite the opposite, in fact. To maintain an attachment to their mothers (because attachment means survival), children will not be able to recognize that their mothers are psychologically unwell because that would be too overwhelming. Instead, children will make themselves the "bad" one who is the cause of their mother's abusive behavior, as that provides them a solution: "Don't be bad and mom won't punish you." Thus, the beginning of shame.

When children assign themselves as the reason for their parents' abuse, it protects them from having to face the extraordinarily scary reality that their parents are unavailable, cruel, and abusive for reasons outside of the child's control. A child cannot face that reality without completely collapsing psychologically. Instead, she makes the abuse, cruelty, and neglect about something she is causing, which places the situation back in her control, where she believes she can do something about it. All of this is happening unconsciously, but over time the narrative solidifies to the point where her self-perception is dramatically skewed and tailored to fit the belief that she is always coming up short. Healthy self-development gets paralyzed in early childhood when the required nutrients for growth are blocked by the constant fear that mom will abandon or reject her.

---

101. Ashley, *Shame-Informed Therap*, 27.
102. Ashley, *Shame-Informed Therapy*, 28.

What would a healthy adult who is observing this type of dyad say? If we don't tell the child that she's the bad one, what is the truth of this situation?

Let's look at the shaming messages you were told versus what ought to have occurred.

I'll start with a list of messages that you may have taken in and we'll compare that to what a healthy parent interaction should look like.

You say: "That hurt my feelings."

A shaming mother says: "Too bad. Your feelings don't matter to me."

A non-shaming mother says: "Aw, I'm sorry that I hurt your feelings. Let's talk about it."

You say: "I want to be a ballerina when I grow up."

A shaming mother says: "You're too fat to do that. And plus, you're not a good dancer anyway."

A non-shaming mother says: "Oh cool! Let's sign you up for ballet classes." OR if affordability is an issue, a healthy response could look like: "I know you do, honey. And what a beautiful dancer you are! I wish we could sign you up for classes, but we can't right now."

You say: "Can I have a sleepover with my friends?"

A shaming mother says: "Why would they want to have a sleepover with you? You're not popular."

A non-shaming mother says: "Of course! I do need you to finish your homework first, okay?"

Appropriate boundaries and limits are important here too. Not all healthy parental responses need to sound like unwavering support regardless of the situation; it's about being realistic, kind, and befitting for the circumstances at hand.

◗ EXERCISE: TALKING TO THE SHAME

Sometimes our logical mind jumps in with its narrative about why we shouldn't feel whatever emotion is coming up and begins to minimize the experience. In other cases, you may be reacting to something from the past that's being infused with the present moment. Here are some questions to ask yourself:

What is my body remembering in these instances?

....

....

....

....

Why does it make perfect sense that I would feel angry? Sad? Scared?

....

....

....

What cues of safety can I take in that bring my body back to a state of calm?

....

....

....

Human beings naturally want things to be simple. We have a tendency toward thinking in all-or-nothing, either/or terms that allow us to categorize our experiences. The problem with this kind of thinking is that it betrays the nuances of reality and can lead to or exacerbate symptoms of anxiety and depression. The either/or mentality is great when we're feeling great. It reinforces the sense of being all-good and impervious to pain, at least in the moment.

Life does not operate in all or nothing terms. You needn't look far to see that contradictions abound and nuance colors everything. When we embrace the fact that multiple things can be true at once, we can then hold space for all parts of us that exist, and live in harmony with both/and reasoning. Therapist Patti Ashley has an exercise that I will adapt here (you can find her version on her website at https://pattiashley.com/emotional-skill-builders/), inviting us to step into paradox, where two truths can coexist, getting us out of the all-or-nothing mindset. This exercise is meant to help us register the contradictory nature of being a human being. When you can live in harmony with paradox, you have nothing to be in conflict about. This can be useful to practice when you're experiencing shame, as it gets us out of one-dimensional thinking.

◗◖ EXERCISE: OPPOSING TRUTHS

For this exercise, I'd like you to write out two opposing truths you can experience simultaneously. Here are some examples:

- I love my partner(s). I get angry at them.
- I hate waking up in the morning. I love having early morning coffee.
- I am angry at my mother. I long to connect with her.
- My children are my everything. They piss me off when they don't listen to me.

You get the idea.

◗ EXERCISE: INTERNAL DIALOGUE

Another exercise I'd like you to try is one in which you have a dialogue between the self-supporting part of you that wants you to be free of shame and the part that took on the shame. You can either do this below or in a journal, using a different color pen/pencils to take on each part of yourself, or you can simply do it as a dialogue in your mind or out loud.

When the part who no longer wishes to be consumed with shame steps forward, what does she say? What does this part want?

....

....

....

....

What does the part who took on the shame say?

....

....

....

And the other part? How would she like to remind the shame part of what's different now?

....

....

....

Keep this going for just a few minutes and see what comes up. I invite you to take a nonjudgmental stance toward the part of you that took on the shaming beliefs, while maintaining a firm connection to the part of you that wants more freedom to live outside of the confining walls of shame.

If things start to get stirred up in such a way that it's no longer tolerable or safe to continue, please stop and take a break. Use one or all of your five senses to bring you back into this space. What do you see? Name three things. What are you hearing right now? Try to name two things. What smells are you aware of? Describe what you're feeling physically (i.e., the chair supporting your legs, your shirt tickling your arm). What do you taste?

Take a moment to engage with something that feels calm and relaxing, or invites your mind to shift focus.

If you still want to engage in a dialogue between these two parts of yourself, please do so. I invite you to also do this with a therapist if the experience becomes overwhelming.

Separating from Shame

Shame is about being exposed in some way that would be perceived as disgraceful, disgusting, wrong, and unworthy of care or understanding. This last piece is an important qualifier: unworthy of care or understanding. It's one thing to feel exposed; it's quite another to be cast out of the tribe. When we are experiencing the excruciating sensations associated with shame, it becomes very difficult to separate from it. In the moment, you feel shame and there's no differentiating yourself from it: I *am* the shame. I *am* bad. The truth, however, is that you are a human experiencing pain. You are not the pain itself, because if that were true, you would have no other experiences. How do we help ourselves out when we're in the grip of this powerful affect?

Feeling Compassion for the Cost of Shame

"Ugh, I know what's coming. Not this again," Mary said to me, with eyes shut and a grimace across her face.

"Not what again?" I asked, confused.

"This self-compassion bullcrap. I don't need to be more compassionate to myself," she replied with a final slump of her shoulders.

"Mary, you don't need to be more of anything. I wonder what gets stirred up for you when you think about being more self-compassionate. Let's make room for that." I wanted to see what she associated with self-compassion, a term that has become over used and ubiquitous as self-care.

BREAK FREE FROM NARCISSISTIC MOTHERS

"I just…I don't know how to do it, or what it even means. The word literally doesn't make sense to me. And then I feel like I'm totally failing you and failing at therapy. Which then makes the shame come right back up."

I was stunned. Trying to be kinder to herself led her to feel more shame, which took her into a hopeless place.

"Mary, I'm so glad you told me this. No wonder you had that reaction! If self-compassion only leads to more shame, why would you want any part in that? I see how valiantly you have been trying to protect yourself from getting too close to shame."

Her desire to protect herself from the vicious forces of shame was actually coming from a very self-caring part of herself—she just didn't know it yet.

"When we start exploring ways to separate from shame, naturally being self-compassionate comes to mind, yet we're both seeing how easy it is for shame to slip itself back into the mix. When you think about attempting to be self-compassionate, you recoil as if it will be yet another thing you'll fail at. I wonder, how do you feel for yourself as you witness the way in which this shame tortures you?"

Mary began to cry. "I feel so sad for myself and angry at this shame. I want it to stop bothering me so much! Why can't I just be free of it?" In between sobs, Mary recalled a time when her mother publicly humiliated her when she was 10 years old. Every year her school held a talent show for the students to perform in. To facilitate more student involvement, the school allowed each student to showcase with an adult if they wanted the extra moral support. Mary's mom jumped on the opportunity. For years, her mom had always boasted about her time being a ballerina when she was younger, and would find subtle ways of jabbing Mary for not being as thin or graceful as she. Mary liked to dance, and so thought that doing a dance routine with her mom would be fun. They spent weeks rehearsing, and on the day of the show, her mom changed the routine. Not only that, but she wore scantily clad attire, emphasizing her long legs, and took center stage while Mary attempted to follow along to the very changed choreography. When she told her mom how much that hurt her, Mary's mom told her that maybe if she were a better dancer she would have picked up on the moves better. For weeks after that, Mary couldn't shake the experience from her mind, and noticed how differently some of the students treated her. From that point on, she no longer allowed herself to be exposed in any way and stopped engaging in social or extracurricular events.

When Mary brought this up in our session, she connected to a deep sympathy and compassion for her little self who only wanted to dance with her mom, and so much anger toward the mother that betrayed her little girl's trust and confidence. We began making room for these feelings.

"Does that little girl deserve to be punished like this?" I asked Mary, in reference to the shaming force inside.

"No. Not at all. I just want to hold her and rock her and tell her that she didn't do anything wrong."

"Would you say that's showing compassion for yourself? That when you see how damaging the shame is to yourself and that little girl, you want to draw a line between you and it?" I asked.

After a few moments Mary said, "I do. I don't want to live with this shame. But how do I do it?"

"Is the shame operating right now?"

"No."

"Then you're already doing it. This compassion you feel and desire to no longer live under that long shadow of shame is helping you connect to a part of you that lives outside of it."

If we are to unwrap ourselves from the poisonous grip of shame, it's important that we know where to start, and to call out our shame any time it shows up. Even labeling it—"Ah, this is shame"—a starting point. Knowing when we're in a shame state helps us see it for what it is, and while the pain is real, the suffering doesn't have to be prolonged. Toxic shame may invite us deeper into its clutches by reinforcing negative self-judgments, turning our attention to the places inside of ourselves that feel deficient. We may even find ourselves fanning the flames of shame by self-isolating, self-harming in some way, or buying into its message as truth. The reality is that shame is universal: all people have felt and will feel its sting from time to time, some more than others. And this has nothing to do with one's deservedness to feel shame. No one deserves to feel shame, especially when it becomes a belief about oneself. Helping ourselves out of shame requires first our desire to do so and then a commitment towards treating ourselves with compassion and care.

Questioning Your Inner Critic

Sarah Peyton, a renowned leader in self-compassion and neurobiology, writes extensively on the ways in which our default way of relating to ourselves can cause significant suffering. In her book *Your Resonant Self*, Peyton offers a new perspective for how we speak to ourselves, one she refers to as the resonant self-witness (RSW). Peyton states, "The RSW is the experience of feeling supported and held. In the brain, it shows up as an easy self-supportive dialogue between the prefrontal cortex (PFC) and the amygdala/limbic system, which has the effect of shifting the savage and traumatized default mode network (DMN), the automatic voice of self-hate and self-recrimination, into the self-accompaniment of a kind, resonant DMN."[103] Essentially what this RSW can do is tap into self-warmth and create a presence of *being with*, even when we're in the depths of despair and hopelessness.

When shame takes the form of bitter self-contempt, fear, or anticipation of the rejection of others, or through critical thoughts like "I'm so stupid; I'll never get this right," pay attention to what happens to the part of you that is being given this treatment. What would you notice, if you could shine a light on the part that is getting shamed? How does this part feel when it is spoken to in this way? Does this part feel like it needs to shrink even more? Does it want to run away and obliterate everything in its path? Would it rather be treated differently? If you could separate yourself from the shame-turned-bully, would it bring you closer to the outcome you're looking for?

When you're stuck and perhaps unable to identify what you need or feel, Peyton offers a suggestion for getting curious with ourselves using what she calls empathy guesses. When we're using empathy guesses with ourselves, we're attempting to be gentle and curious. A simple example of this would be to use the framework, "Would you like some

acknowledgment of _____?

And do you need _____?"

For instance, if you're experiencing shame or a sense of hopelessness, fear, or inferiority, you might ask yourself: "Do you need acknowledgment for how big the world feels to you right now? And are you needing some space to define yourself a little more?" Consider what happens when you ask yourself a question like this. Do you notice something soften-ing or opening up more? Do you yearn for more of these kinds of questions? Do you need acknowledgment for how scary it is to be seen sometimes? Are you needing to know that you're not alone in this after all?

In a similar way, Peyton suggests asking our critical parts what they are most longing for. Is this inner voice longing for something on your behalf? For instance, "Are you longing to protect me from embarrassment? Do you worry that I will blunder and create disconnection with the people I need closeness from?" This type of inquiry moves us out of self-judgment and into the heart of the need we are attempting to meet. We are less likely to find peace

---

103. Sarah Peyton, *Your Resonant Self: Guided Meditations and Exercises to Engage Your Brain's Capacity for Healing* (New York: W.W. Norton & Company, 2017), 45.

or resolution if we're chronically caught in right or wrong, all or nothing, or dichotomous thinking about our feelings or needs.

Our feelings and needs don't like to be met with punishment or coldness, which completely stifle self-expression. This is the equivalent of stepping onto a budding flower pushing its way through the soil; we crush it before it gets a chance to reveal itself to us. When we greet ourselves with warmth and interest, and this includes even our harsh, critical, and unaccepting voice, we can actually see what that part is trying to do for us.[104] Listening only to the words, we miss the deeper meaning and strivings. A cruel self-devaluation may have originated as a need to be considered favorably in a home where only accomplishments and achievements were accepted. Peyton states, "As the inner voices are heard with clarity, people begin to notice that everything they do is an attempt to meet a need."[105]

Third Person Self-Talk

Researchers have found that speaking to ourselves in third person is an emotion regulation skill that diminishes the negative effects of self-condemnation.[106] The way you do this is simple. Begin speaking to yourself, starting with your name at the beginning. Give it a try. I'll start. "Hannah, are you feeling particularly overwhelmed as you write this? Are you needing some support in making your thoughts clearer?" Can you see how this minor detail could create some space between you and what you're experiencing?

The researcher Ethan Kross and others discovered the phenomenon that referring to oneself in the third person allows for greater self-regulation because it creates a degree of separation between oneself and the experience.[107] [108] In the Kross study, the researchers discovered that those who referred to themselves using their names performed better in stress-inducing activities and were able to regulate their thoughts, feelings, and behaviors.[109] When we're regulated, we're less reactive and more likely to respond to both ourselves and others with more understanding.

---

104. Peyton, *Your Resonant Self,* 61.
105. Peyton, *Your Resonant Self,* 76.
106. Brackett, *Permission to Feel,* 152.
107. Ethan Kross, Emma Bruehlman-Senecal, Jiyoung Park, Aleah Burson, Adrienne Dougherty, Holly Shablack, Ryan Bremner, Jason Moser, and Ozlem Ayduk, "Self-Talk as a Regulatory Mechanism: How You Do It Matters," *Journal of Personality and Social Psychology,* 106, no. 2 (2014): 304-24, https://doi.org/10.1037/a0035173.
108. Brackett, *Permission to Feel,* 152.
109. Kross et al., "Self-Talk as a Regulatory Mechanism: How You Do It Matters," 304-24.

BREAK FREE FROM NARCISSISTIC MOTHERS

Can you practice this skill starting now? Let's say you have to go see your mom later today and are dreading the thought of it. Practice speaking to yourself using your first name at the beginning of each sentence, and notice what you're experiencing in the process.

Survival Mechanisms

In families where one (or both) parents is a narcissist with high expectations or specific and unreachable standards, a child will learn to regulate both herself and her narcissistic parent by revealing the parts of her she thinks are "good" and hiding the parts she believes are "bad." This tragically creates a split between her more authentic self and the false self she has to display to her parents. Narcissistic mothers have been living this way for most of their lives: split up, discarding their "less than" selves in favor of a polished persona that walls off pain and shame.

Shame can be thought of as a survival emotion in that it keeps us connected to others. When shame is operating in a healthy range, we can take the message of shame and course-correct our actions. Healthy shame regulates our actions so that we don't violate societal norms. When we feel healthy shame, we make changes to our behavior, apologize when necessary, and move forward in our lives. Shame that turns self-abusive, however, perpetuates the belief that we simply are wrong, unlovable, and unworthy, and that no one could or would accept us.

Survival mechanisms, or ways in which we preserve our relationships with others, typically start from an early age. If your mother was not safe to be around, you likely adapted to her unsafe behaviors by silencing any part of yourself that could potentially unleash her wrath. Let's imagine your story of self-silencing as a scene from a fantasy novel. The hero enters a deep, dark cave in which she must not wake the sleeping dragon, lest she wants to face a mouthful of sharp teeth and a belly full of fire. The hero would go to great lengths to make sure she does not make any noise: holding her breath, taking a longer route, shrinking her body to slip through cracks, and deftly managing her footfalls. No matter what, she cannot wake the sleeping dragon. Her survival depends on it. You had to find your own self-silencing techniques too. What were they?

◖ REFLECTION

Take a moment here to write out all the ways in which you silenced yourself so as not to provoke your mother. What aspects of yourself did you have to deny in order to please her?

How would you like to reclaim those denied aspects so that they no longer have to be punished or ignored? Would you like to give your voice the freedom to express itself?

How Does Shame Start?

Shame-informed therapist and researcher Patricia DeYoung describes the advent of shame, stating, "A child has to have at least one caregiver who is able to respond in an attuned, consistent way to what the child feels. If this is missing in a major way, the child will translate the distress of the mismatch into a feeling like, 'I can't make happen what I need...so there's something wrong with me.'"[110]

Children who cannot get their emotional or physical needs met by their caregivers must suppress their longing for love and connection as a means of self-preservation.[111] [112] When this happens over and over again, children learn to suppress their needs and attempt to get

---

110. DeYoung, *Understanding and Treating Chronic Shame*, 5-6.
111. Lowen, *Narcissism*, 190.
112. DeYoung, *Understanding and Treating Chronic Shame*, 6.

them met in a different way. Eventually, the ways in which children attempt to get their needs met turn into maladaptive coping strategies. These maladaptive strategies only offer temporarily relief. These strategies are attempts at covering the sense of emptiness or fear of being unworthy, but over time stop being useful. Soon a new strategy must be found.

Children have to be resilient against abuse. Since they do not have the tools adults have to protect themselves, they are at the mercy of their own psychological defense system. In a time of great distress, these defenses are lifesaving and serve as attempts to become regulated again. Unfortunately, the protective strategies that were used in childhood and adolescence don't work as well in adulthood. At a certain point, these protective mechanisms begin to lose their effectiveness, and often more extreme versions are required in order to regulate.

Protective mechanisms might look like the following:

- Avoidance
- Addiction: sex, drugs, alcohol, shopping
- Dissociation
- Intellectualization
- Distraction
- Minimization of pain
- Serial relationships
- Fights
- Withdrawal and/or shutdown
- Ceased contact with others
- Isolation

It's important to recognize that these protective mechanisms may feel like our most immediate solution to reduce pain. Let's not view these mechanisms as right or wrong, but more from the perspective of finding the wound underneath that is needing protection. As an adult, you now have an opportunity to truly attend to that wound in ways you didn't as a child. Working with a therapist is one of those ways. Through the healing dynamics of a therapeutic relationship, you can begin healing early childhood experiences of trauma, shame, and pain in a caring relationship. This type of therapy is akin to reparenting ourselves. We get to have a new kind of experience in a relationship that allows for all parts of the self to be seen and welcomed.

This type of emotional healing results from being in a therapeutic relationship that helps us contextualize our early childhood experiences, offering a space where all feelings and needs can be held with positive regard. From this type of a relationship a person can forge new ways of relating to themselves and others that contribute to a wider sense of wellbeing.

Tactics of a Narcissist

I'd like to devote this section to outlining how a narcissist may use shame to coerce you into feeling small and unworthy. Sadly, many cult leaders are highly narcissistic and use similar shaming tactics against their own followers. Narcissism expert Julie Hall describes the coercive tactics narcissists use to get others to comply with their will:

1. **Isolation:** "removing the target's independence, such as by restricting contact with friends, outside family, and social connections; constraining physical freedom; and limiting financial resources.

2. **Removal Of Free Will:** destabilizing the target's fundamental sense of self, reality, and worldview through persistent questioning and negative judgment.

3. **Instilled Powerlessness:** undermining the target's confidence in her/his thoughts, feelings, and perceptions through distortions of reality, gaslighting, and dismissing and denying truths and facts to cause self-doubt and cognitive dissonance.

4. **Thought Control:** controlling acceptable opinion and expression in the target through interrogation, judgment, intimidation, rejection and unspoken rules of engagement.

5. **Terror:** controlling the target's words, actions, and thoughts through implied, threatened, or real verbal, physical, and/or sexual violence, often combined with intermittent repentance, promises of change, and/or rewards to keep the target in the game and hold out hope for change."[113]

I will now add the ways in which I believe you can utilize the opposite tactics to return back to yourself and stay connected to your own truth.

1. **Connection:** Remind yourself that staying connected to individuals, communities, organizations, loved ones, clubs, and neighbors is part of your recovery plan. When we're connected with others, we are reminded of the wider world that exists, and that takes us out of an isolated state. Staying connected in this way can increase our resilience against stressors and conflict. Since you are an adult, you get to do things differently now, and as a result your mother should not have open access to your

---

113. Hall, *The Narcissist in Your Life*, 60.

physical space, finances, phone numbers of important people in your life (unless you have given her access to numbers in case of an emergency), or your daily schedule. If right now your mother has access to any of these, and you no longer wish for this, please make a plan to remove her access.

2. **Honoring Your Free Will:** You are an autonomous being. You get to decide what to wear, whom to talk to, and how you will manage your energy. Your power comes from recognizing that you are in charge of you and get to determine your life. We are powerful when we are connected, but more than that, we are powerful when we are in relationship to the choices we have. As noted in Julie Hall's list, your mom will endeavor to question your decisions in a way that causes you to doubt yourself. This is partially her unconscious attempt at usurping your free will. Start approaching your self-doubt with this understanding in mind. You may feel a familiar pull to fall back in line, however you will not do that this time. Instead, you will hold yourself with dignity and stay committed to your boundaries. You cannot be cowed when you are fully anchored to your truth.

3. **Reclaiming Powerfulness:** Similar to honoring your free will, reclaiming your power is like making the choice to never turn your back on yourself. It's the equivalent of meeting the part of you that has felt powerless, pulling her up off the floor, and having her back. You don't give away your power to anyone anymore. Being "in your power" really translates to accompanying yourself with presence and having the freedom to choose *how* you show up. There is no need to justify yourself to your mother anymore. That ship has sailed. She is not the gatekeeper to your wellbeing. You will let your body inform you, using physical sensations, emotions, or impulses to guide you in knowing your reality; gaslighting cannot thrive when we trust ourselves.

4. **Thought Liberation:** Thoughts, opinions, and expressions are all subjective experiences for the most part. Our thoughts can contain ideas, facts, abstract concepts, images, dreams, and miscellaneous data that are outside of our control. We get to choose whether or not we express them. Our thoughts and ideas belong to us, and we get to decide how they influence our lives. No one person can ever tell you what you are allowed to think or believe. Only you can do that.

5. **Boundaries:** Our boundaries are our peace, our liberation, and our home. When we are rooted—that is, firm and resilient against the winds of narcissism—we are truly able to choose how we respond and where we place ourselves in relation to the narcissist. How we respond to ourselves is of the utmost importance. Here is a mantra for you: "Within this space, no one can threaten me without facing the consequences of their actions. I can choose to leave, distance myself, and maintain consistency of boundaries within my own mind and body. No one can manipulate me when I am honoring myself

and my truth. Terror is not something I allow into my life anymore." You might want to memorize this mantra.

These are skills to practice every day; the more you engage with them, the more real they become.

Your Plan of Action

If you are still communicating with or seeing your mother, I'd like for you to create a plan of action for after you see her, especially if you are anticipating that the visit will be challenging in some way. Schedule in self-care or rest after the interaction. If your mother tends to bogart your time, make the commitment to be done interacting with her by a certain time so that you have the rest of the day available to do you. Make the time following your interaction with her nourishing and supportive. Give yourself exactly what you need.

Can you practice this skill starting now?

Let's say you have to go see your mom later today and are dreading the thought of it. How might you speak to yourself from a place that is encouraging? Try using your first name at the beginning of each sentence and acknowledge what you're needing. It would sound like: "Self, are you feeling agitated by the idea of seeing mom today? Do you need to know that you'll get through this and have time for yourself after?" What do you notice experiencing when you speak to yourself in this way?

Easing Out of Shame

As you've seen, shame can be a highly dysregulating experience and can lead to profound deficits in how we view ourselves. When the nervous system believes that you are in danger well beyond fight or flight, it will signal the freeze response, also known as "playing dead." When we're in a freeze state, we're likely to see the world through a lens of hopelessness. Shame often emerges from this is viewpoint if we are chronically frozen.

If you are experiencing a nervous system freeze state, you are likely to have thoughts that sound like this:

- "I'll never amount to anything."
- "What's the point?"
- "I'll never get any better and my partner will leave me."
- "There is no one and nowhere that is safe."
- "I'm completely alone in this."

This way of thinking is the direct result of your nervous system telegraphing a particular kind of danger to the mind and body. It's going to feel and sound differently from fight or flight. When you are perceiving danger, your mind will tell the story of danger. When you are out of perceived or real danger and back into safety, your mind will tell the story of safety.[114] Remember that this shame is a story of the mind. Imagine if you wore sunglasses all day without realizing it. What would the world look like? Might things seem a bit dark and dim? How would you feel and think about the world you're living in with these sunglasses on? Would you feel motivated and energized or depleted and tired?

◗ EXERCISE: EASING OUT OF SHAME

When you're experiencing shame, ask yourself some of these questions so that you might start to ease out of the experience.

Am I the only one in the world going through this right now? Is it possible that others have experienced this painful shame too?

---

114. Deb Dana, *Polyvagal Exercises for Safety and Connection: 50 Client-Centered Practices,* 23.

Do I have a skewed way of seeing myself that has led to this shame?

Am I thinking about this situation or myself in either/or concepts? Either I'm all good or I'm all bad? Have I forgotten to include context in the way I'm thinking about myself or the situation?

What would the part of me that's feeling this shame long to hear from someone who's been through this situation too?

Can you separate yourself enough to witness that this shame is only an experience rather than a truth?

If you continue to find yourself paralyzed by shame, it's important to recognize a few gentle and self-supportive actions you can take to be with yourself in a loving way. You don't have to squash the shame before you take care of yourself. Simply notice the feeling, name it, and take an action that supports your mind or body. Here is a list of ideas in case you're feeling a bit stuck.

- Do some breath work. Try breathing in for four counts, holding your breath for four, and breathing out for four counts. Do this over the course of 1–2 minutes.

- Perform a restorative yoga sequence or invigorating vinyasa (a string of different yoga poses performed one after another).

- Go for a walk in nature and use all five of your senses to anchor into the moment.

- Mourn for the part of yourself that is in pain and then journal about the experience, making sure to include compassionate self-talk, the context of the situation, and curiosity about the experience, with as little self-judgment as you can manage.

- Talk to someone you trust about the shame. Ask if they can simply listen and reflect back to you what you're saying. If you and they are open to it, inquire if they've ever experienced shame like this. Let this be an opportunity to feel connected to others.

- Do a loving kindness meditation.

- Remind yourself that *all* feelings eventually pass. Shame is simply a passenger in this moment.

Chapter 8

COMMUNICATION AND NO CONTACT

Communication is foundational to any and all relationships. It is the nutrient-dense soil needed for a healthy garden to grow. We rely on our words to convey what we need and how we feel in relationship to other people. When the soil is starved of nutrients, the garden can't grow, and our desires for something beautiful end up frustrated. Without clear communication we lose something essential to our connection with others and our relationships flounder.

Most of us were taught the basics of communicating as children in school: wait your turn before you speak, be nice and polite, don't yell, speak slower, say what you mean. Then we grew up and saw that not many people adhered to these simple constructs. If you're like 99 percent of the population, you learned how to *actually* communicate by watching the people around you. Your parents, grandparents, kids at school, movies, friends, and so forth. What you *really* learned was: talk over the other person to get your point across, yell if necessary, be passive aggressive, speak quickly lest the other person cut you off, be indirect and if others don't take your side, stonewall them.

As a daughter of a narcissistic mother, you know this intimately. You know that communicating with her is a feat of strength and persistence, bordering on what feels like an impossibility. When your mother communicates to you, she uses whatever is at her disposal to get what *she* wants. Her ability to manipulate the storyline to cast herself as the victim/

martyr and you as the persecutor is award winning and oh, so convincing. As a child, you unwittingly took on this role, which put you in the category of the hurtful, inconsiderate, manipulative, mean-spirited, selfish, or stupid person every time. Brilliantly, you found a way to hide your needs, disguise your requests, and play the game so as to keep yourself safe. Back then, these childhood adaptations were what you needed to survive your mother; you don't need them now. As an adult woman, you have what your sweet child self didn't: freedom and choice. You are now permitted to honor your boundaries and engage in clear communication so that you can be protected in a different way.

One thing to keep in mind as you embark on a new pathway of communicating with your mother is that this is not a magic bullet. Being able to assert and express yourself clearly will not change her. The purpose of learning and utilizing the tools to communicate with a narcissistic mother is to help you, not to change her. I know how deeply you want your mother to change; for her to finally realize the damage she has caused (is causing) and finally make amends with you. She won't.

Communicating with a narcissist should not be predicated on the hope that they will see reason or finally see things from your perspective. You would be setting yourself up for immense frustration and disappointment. Nor do you need to qualify or overexplain yourself in order for your perspective to be valid or justified. You are inherently entitled to your needs, boundaries, and choices. When you come to recognize that you are already free to make whatever decisions you need to make, communicating with your mom will be coming from a place of a liberation, rather than from desperation.

There is no secret equation to communicating that will get a narcissist to become more empathetic or to *finally* take ownership of their part in your relationship. However, there is a pathway that is available for you to take that will dramatically alter the way in which you interact with your mother. It requires courage, a commitment to honoring your needs, and the willingness to do something new. At first, being clear, direct, and honest will feel uncomfortable; anything we haven't yet done will feel this way. You've gotten accustomed to traveling a very narrow and rocky road of communication with your mother. On this road, you adapted to silencing certain parts of yourself and keeping them out of the conversation. As you remove the veil of silence from these parts, they will clamor to be heard. Most often, these parts will feel a lot of anger and grief over the ways in which they've been treated. Connecting with these parts is what will help you recognize what it is you are needing.

As you work on improving your communication with your mom, you may notice her reactions changing in range or size. Narcissists who have gotten used to manipulating the people in their lives may resort to retaliation against those who refuse to take their abuse. Your mother will likely up the ante by using more severe strategies to push you out of your boundaries, such as guilt tripping you, inviting you to turn against yourself by taking on the role as the "bad guy," gaslighting you, and flat out ignoring what you're saying. While each daughter will have to determine how much she wants her mother to be part of her life, the painful reality is that she is unlikely to change, and this may require you to reevaluate whether or not you want to remain in contact with her. It's important to recognize at a certain point that going no-contact may be necessary and inevitable. This is not true for every single case, as narcissism runs on a spectrum, but for many adult daughters this is the path that they eventually take.

In communicating with your mom, it's important to establish a few ground rules so that you can go into this prepared. In communicating with a narcissist, I suggest you avoid utilizing the following tactics:

- Name calling
- Using threats to cajole her out of behaviors
- Using vague and overgeneralized statements about her
- Justifying, over-apologizing, rationalizing, explaining, or pleading[115]
- Defensiveness or attempting to convince her of your stance
- Bypassing her and your own boundaries
- Bullying or yelling
- Getting drawn into argument or debates

We will encourage instead the following actions, which aim to enhance your selfhood and the autonomy and sovereignty of your own life. This is where you can draw on your boundaries and state your needs clearly. Try these strategies out:

- Stating what you need, want, and don't want
- Using non-defensive language (*We'll explore this momentarily*)
- Setting healthy limits on how you will interact with her unhealthy behaviors
- Making clear what your boundaries are and following through when they get ignored or bypassed
- Leaving the situation if boundaries continue to be ignored or abusive behavior begins

Setting and communicating your limits with your mother and truly respecting your own boundaries establishes a new rule for yourself: I will protect ME first. What's beautiful about

---

115. Susan Forward. *Mothers Who Can't Love: A Healing Guide for Daughters* (New York: HarperCollins, 2013), 210.

protecting yourself is that you needn't punish your mother in order to do this. Boundaries are really about ourselves and what we need in order to live healthy lives; they're not about changing the behavior of someone else. Rather, setting a boundary is like saying, "Mom, you don't need to change how you see the world or me, but I will change how I show up in our relationship. I will no longer accept abuse, so I will be practicing saying no more often, distancing myself when I need to, and living life according to what serves me best."

Some women, however, may choose to take the no-contact route right off the bat, and that's okay. Going low-contact is another option.

Candice, a woman in her mid-sixties, told me recently that she couldn't fully commit to going no-contact, stating, "I don't know, I don't think I'll ever be ready to go that route. But what I have found is that by giving myself the permission to have healthier boundaries on my time and my interactions with her, I feel more free and true to myself. I know some women really need to go no-contact, but for me I'm realizing that having really good self-care and boundaries with my mom is my golden ticket back to myself." Her solution was to reduce her one-on-one conversations with her mom and instead find ways to interact with her mom in the presence of other people, be it family members, grandchildren, or neighbors.

It was evident that for Candice, her sense of freedom came from knowing that she had options and strategies to use while still maintaining a semblance of connection with her mom. Only it was on her own terms.

Position Statements

Susan Forward, a prominent figure in the narcissism abuse recovery world, suggests in her book *Mothers Who Can't Love: A Healing Guide for Daughters* examples of position statements that clearly articulate what you want and don't want,[116] what you will tolerate and will no longer tolerate. They sound like this:

- "I am no longer willing to...
- I am willing to...
- It's no longer acceptable for you to...
- It's not okay that you...
- I need you to..."[117]

---

116. Susan Forward, *Mothers Who Can't Love: A Healing Guide for Daughters* (New York: HarperCollins, 2013), 210.

117. Forward, *Mothers Who Can't Love*, 210.

Returning to Candice: When she discovered that she could no longer tolerate an intimate relationship with her mother, she had to find a way to express this. If she had just said, "Mom, we're breaking up. I can't be as intimate with you as I used to be," (while not problematic in and of itself) it would have led to her mother's defensive anger, retaliation, and blaming. Instead, Candice tried out one of the above position statements, which sounded like, "Mom, I'm no longer willing to talk about politics with you. I need you to find someone else to discuss your concerns with." You're probably wondering what her mom said next, and you may not be surprised to discover that she completely stonewalled Candice. In our next session Candice brought up what happened.

"I tried the position statement and boy, did my mom not like it."

"Yeah, I can imagine she wasn't expecting that, huh? How was it for you to simply state your position?" I asked.

"Oh…it was amazing. I felt totally batshit scared at first, but after I said it, I felt empowered. I thought it was going to feel worse after, but I actually felt relatively calm," she marveled with confidence.

"And how did she take it?" I wondered.

"Not well. I mean, she did her typical song and dance of protesting and telling me how she actually doesn't talk my ear off about politics. But I remembered that my job is not to convince her to stop doing what she does; rather, I kept in mind that all I'm doing is changing my relationship to it. So that felt good. But after that, she just went silent. At first, I thought she hung up. But no, she was silent and letting me know. So, I gently said, 'okay, well I'm going to go. I'll talk to you later, mom.' and I hung up. I didn't hear from her for four weeks. I knew she was punishing me."

In previous sessions, Candice had told me that reactions like that from her mother would often leave her feeling wracked with guilt and shame. I wondered if that was happening for her now, so I asked, "And when you knew she was punishing you, what feelings were you having?"

"At first, I felt that familiar guilt, like I had done something wrong. I could even feel the impulse to want to pick up the phone and apologize to her, but I stopped myself. I said, 'Candice, you are doing something new. It's okay for her to have feelings about what you said. It's not okay that she's trying to punish you like this, but you don't have to take the bait. Remember, you are allowed to have needs and boundaries.' I even have that as a post-it note on my computer, in my car, and a reminder on my phone. It's not easy to remember that on my own, so having reminders help. But damn, I'm so glad that I'm really leaning into it."

It's so important for you to remember that having healthy communication with your mother is more about you upholding your boundaries than it is about getting her to engage in healthy communication. She's going to respond with her typical defenses and it's your job to make sure you stay true to *you*, and resist the pull to keep yourself small. This takes practice, patience with yourself, and a lot of self-compassion. The point of building healthier communication strategies is to serve you; not in a self-centered, at-the-expense-of-every-one-else kind of way, but from a place of self-respect.

Susan Forward states, "By changing your behavior, you're creating an atmosphere in which she will either change hers slowly or demonstrate to you that she's unwilling to change."[118] A powerful statement, indeed.

Statements to avoid: "you always" or "you never."

As tempting as these two phrases are (and as real as they may be), they are going to get you nowhere. If you are attempting to have some kind of relationship with your mother, being explicit and specific in how you communicate will help you to avoid these generalizations. This does not mean that you need to spill your guts to her, but it does mean you have to either speak up or take action when it matters. "You always" or "you never" is vague and overgeneralizing to the point where it loses its meaning for the other person. It is more likely to cause an alarm bell of shame to go off, and for a narcissist it's going to be more like a tidal wave of shame that will be defended against faster than a bullet train. When a narcissist is in a defense, game over. When you are specific, clear, and willing to honor your needs and boundaries? Game on.

Statements to use: "I am no longer willing to..." or "I need you to..."

Consider for a moment imagining a typical conversation with your mom, except this time imagine her words coming out of a six-year-old. How does it hit you differently? Is it comical? Do you feel calm in the presence of this child or are you enraged and trying to keep it all together?

The reason I'm suggesting this is to show you that in reality your mother is operating from a developmentally young place. While your mother is older than you are, with more life experience, this doesn't mean much when she's been emotionally stunted. In fact, suggesting you imagine her as a six-year-old may be giving too much credit in terms of maturity. Many who study narcissism believe that it is equivalent to the developmental maturity of a two-year-old.

---

118. Forward, *Mothers Who Can't Love,* 216.

When a child is throwing a tantrum, angry because they want something and you are not allowing them to have it, or conversely, they want you to look at a finger painting they did in class, they are doing this to serve a need to feel validated. For a child, this is totally harmless and part of their development. Life is about them, and that's by design for their survival. When a narcissist has a need to be validated, part of their strategy will be about invalidating you. On an emotional-development front, a narcissist and a two-year-old will present very similarly, except a narcissist does not grow out of this phase like a two-year-old does.

How you set boundaries with a two-year-old or a seventy-year-old narcissist will likely remain consistent. When either uses language that is hurtful, acts in a way that's disrespectful or inconsiderate, it is our job to assert what our boundaries are.

Sharon Ellison, in her book *Taking the War Out of Our Words: The Art of Powerful Non-Defensive Communication*, describes non-defensive communication as the equivalent of taking a rifle off one's shoulder, stating, "To put down the rifle means I don't have to defend myself anymore."[119] Gabor Maté, trauma expert, describes something similar in the way individuals get triggered, comparing it to being a loaded weapon ready to explode.[120] Triggers merely reflect to us the part of ourselves that is holding onto trauma, resentment, and judgment. We don't need to avoid triggers so much as we need to be with the part of us that is in pain.

It only makes sense that there is a part in you that wants to explode when you think of all the ways your mom has hurt, devalued, and insulted you. As satisfying as it is to imagine blowing up at her and unloading all the things you want to say to her, in reality it would keep you stuck in a pain cycle with her. Your words would only get lost, distorted, and twisted up by her narcissistic point of view. In the end her defenses will reign supreme. This type of explosive rage that, in fantasy, feels satisfying, in reality only leads to more disappointment, hurt, and anger.

However, the point is not to stifle your anger or self-expression, but give it a different path to travel. We can honor your anger by giving it a healthy form of expression so that it doesn't have to look or feel like a rifle ready to fire; instead, it can be more like a commanding general that embodies confidence and only needs the right words and follow-through to be effective. And this isn't about communicating ever so perfectly, but finding a pathway where your words can be powerful all on their own and your actions can keep yourself in integrity.

---

119. Sharon Strand Ellison, *Taking the War Out of Our Words: The Art of Powerful Non-Defensive Communication* (Berkeley: Bay Tree Publishing, 2002), xvii.
120. Gabor Maté, "Compassionate Inquiry" (Training Course), January 2019.

◖ REFLECTION

What are some ways I can communicate non-defensively with my mom?

What are my fears about communicating with her in this way?

If I could stay connected to my boundaries and use my words to convey my limits, how would this impact my self-esteem and my interactions with my mom?

What happens when I imagine making clear statements to my mom about what I will or will not tolerate and following through with my boundaries? Do I feel my own strength? Does it feel scary and vulnerable?

You may be thinking, "I can't practice being non-defensive with my mom because she's a narcissist! I have to defend myself." I can't argue with you there, because in many ways you're right. However, let's consider the nuances between *self-defense* and *defensiveness*. The act of becoming defensive suggests that we are disconnected from our source of power and are using everything in our arsenal to get them to stand down or to make them afraid of us. Defensiveness suggests that we have bypassed what our emotions are telling us and are using something less effective to express ourselves.

Defending oneself or acting in self-defense suggests a desire to protect and honor the self. When we're in this place, we needn't get caught in ceaseless arguments or stay in a situation that is unsafe or causes psychological harm. We can be empowered to engage the other person from a place of integrity. Let's explore how this would actually look.

Before Eden even sat down, she looked at me and said, "You'll never guess what happened yesterday. I actually practiced being non-defensive with my mom and my sister and I felt so powerful!"

"That is wonderful, Eden! Tell me more," I inquired.

"Well, my mom started doing her typical routine about how I never consider her feelings and my sister chimed in and told me about how selfish she always thought I was. It was the perfect storm of feeling totally attacked and defensive. I noticed the part of me that started to bristle and wanted to attack back. Instead, I remembered that I don't have to engage in this kind of behavior anymore, so instead of doing my usual 'here's why you're wrong and I'm a good person' clap back, I decided to say, 'It looks like we won't be able to have a healthy conversation right now. When you're ready to speak to me with more respect, I'll be available to hear it.'"

"Woah, Eden! What a tremendous moment for you. How did it feel to practice this way of dialoguing with them? I know this is so new, huh?"

"Honestly, I couldn't have asked for a better moment to practice this. I realized that they were inviting me back into an old cycle that I've participated in since I was eight. It felt so incredible to both my adult self and that little eight-year-old me to simply bow out grace-fully. Of course, I wanted to tell them both off, but I resisted and reminded myself that I just don't have to engage. I didn't need to justify or explain myself. So instead, I decided to cease fire and leave the battlefield."

Eden defended herself by stopping a harmful conversation that used to make her feel help-less and defensive. In this case, Eden's self-defense showed up in the form of self-respect and self-empowerment. Another framework to consider in describing the difference between reacting defensively versus acting in self-defense is that the former is like being put on your heels, whereas the latter is having your feet planted firmly in the ground.

Statements to avoid: "You're a narcissist" or "You have a personality disorder."

If it's not obvious by now, calling your mom a narcissist or telling her she has personality disorder is only going to reinforce her existing narcissism and/or personality disorder. Because of their high degree of shame and their fear of being seen as "weak" or inferior, calling a narcissist a narcissist is not going to take you anywhere. The shame that they work so hard to avoid will awaken, and they will need to rely on whatever it takes to stop the threat to their sense of self. Essentially, "you" statements tend to do the opposite of what we want, leading the other to counter with an even bigger attack. In addition, these statements make it about the other person, whereas in non-defensive and non-violent communication, the aim is to communicate what *you* need.

Consider a time in your life when you might have wanted to tell your mom, "You're a narcissist." What were you likely feeling? What was happening in the moment between the two of you? Were you experiencing a sense of being overpowered by her, angry, small and helpless, bossed around, diminished? What were you hoping a statement like that would stop her from doing? What would have happened if you had said that? Would it have worked?

Statements to use: "It's not okay that you..." or "It's not acceptable that you..."

These statements bypass the need to call her a name and instead put you back in a position of authority over what is acceptable for you. They help to define your boundaries and allow you to be specific about what you will or won't accept. Not only are you giving context to her, which does matter, you are also being specific in what follows. For instance, let's take a typical interaction that Christine would have with her mom *before* she discovered new tools for communicating. It went a little something like this.

Mom: Are you coming home for Thanksgiving this year? Your aunt will be so devastated if you don't. You know how much she sacrifices in order to be here.

Christine: Yes, mom. I'll be there. I might not be able to arrive a week before like last year. Work has been crazy.

Mom: Well, you better explain that to your aunt because she is coming a week early this year. Do you not think about how other people might feel?

Christine: Mom, I don't know what you want me to say. I can't arrive early like I told you because of work. I can't change that.

Mom: I can't believe you! I thought you knew how important this was to me. I go through so much to prepare the food, the house, and even my weight! (*Notice how before it was her aunt who wanted this?*) Did you know I lost five pounds this month? I want to look good for everyone and you coming late makes everything worse.

Christine: Honestly, mom? I think you're a narcissist and you need to get help.

Mom: You know what? Don't come. You are officially uninvited. If I see you here, I'll call the police.

This went downhill fast. Now, before we start to dissect it, let's extend some care toward Christine, who truly felt bombarded and attacked by her mother. It's natural that when we are being attacked we want to either concede to get the abuse to stop or retaliate to hurt the other person back. Christine was often stuck between these two places. When we talked, I was struck by how much Christine wanted to please her mom as a means of reducing her mother's outbursts. Christine was stuck between a desire to be assertive and an old fear from childhood of her mother overpowering her. It became clear that Christine wanted to find a way out of getting caught in these traps with her mom, so we focused on helping her build skills around disengaging rather than getting stuck deeper in conflict.

How to Disengage

1. Keep It About You

This is a funny thing to say when we're talking about narcissism I realize, but there is a difference here. If we look at Christine's interaction, her mother came out swinging and was not interested in seeing things from Christine's perspective. Naturally, Christine felt frustrated and did what anyone who's cornered would do: fought back. When I say keep it about you, what I mean is make your boundaries, needs, and limits clear to yourself before you engage with your mother. Every time she tries to bring the focus back to herself or how you're disappointing her, bring your focus back to what your boundaries are and stick to them. You needn't justify them, simply state them as facts.

We build boundaries by naming what we feel, what we need, and what we plan to do to honor the two.

For this exercise, we'll stick with making our needs and boundaries clear and explicit. The formula, if you will, lies below. Let's take Christine and see if we can identify what she would like to say using this strategy.

I feel _____

when you _____.

I will not _____ with you.

If you _____,

I will _____.

When you _____

I feel _____.

I will not _____ with you.

If you _____,

I will _____.

"I feel angry when you insult my choices. I will not continue to have this conversation with you. If you continue to insult me, I will hang up."

Another could be:

"When you speak to me like this, I feel angry. I will not discuss this with you right now. If you would like to call me later to discuss this differently, I will be available next Sunday."

2. Follow Through on Your Statements

If you've used the above formula and your mother continues to bombard you with messages, assaulting you with more questions or threats, or even attempting to pull you back in an argument, it's important that you not give any more to her. You may decide to follow up by saying, "I will not be discussing this with you right now and I'll be turning my phone off," but I recommend that be the only thing you follow up with. Where adult daughters can feel stuck is when they try the above, but continue to engage with their mothers. This sends a mixed message to both parties: I won't talk to you anymore, but I'll keep talking to you to explain myself.

Examples of following through:

- "If you continue to discuss this with me when I've asked you not to, I will not be responding (or if you're in person: then I will leave)."
- "I'm turning my phone off and won't be available to talk for the remainder of the day."
- "This topic is not up for discussion. I would be happy to talk more about your newly planted garden though. Tell me about that."

- "I understand that's how you feel. If you resort to yelling or insulting me, however, I will leave and be unavailable to talk for the week. If you want to tell me how you feel in a calm manner, then I will listen."

3. Keep Responses Simple and Avoid Over-Explaining or Justifying Your Position

Ellison states, "When we justify our behavior, we put more energy into countering the other person's position than in clearly establishing our own."[121]

Justifying our behavior often feels like slipping on ice. The more we try to wrest control over our feet, the more we slip and flail about. Even the word *justify* means to "show or prove to be right or reasonable," according to the *Oxford Dictionary*. If you have to prove to be right, you've already lost—especially in the face of narcissism. Proving our rightness puts power in the other person, as though they must give the green light of approval. When you get caught in this maneuver, you're actually giving the narcissist more power over your choices and boundaries, even when you mean to do the opposite.

When the intention behind clear communication is to simply state your position, rather than defend, blame, justify, or get the other person to change, you are operating from a place of freedom. Another way to put it is that when you no longer need your mother to be someone that she's not, you don't have to exert so much energy into changing her. Instead, the focus becomes about changing *you* in response to her. You don't need her approval to assert yourself. Your body, mind, personal space, and energy are yours to protect and be in control of.

Susan Forward has a list of non-defensive responses in her book, *Mothers Who Can't Love,* that I have adapted. You can find more in her book on page 200. Here are some examples of non-defensive statements that are simple and to the point. Typically, we use these phrases as brakes in a conversation that is becoming unhealthy or toxic, or getting into the familiar territory of attack-justify.

- I understand.[122]
- You are entitled to believe that. Or: You are entitled to your opinion.[123]
- No, thank you (the broken record technique: continue saying "no, thank you" as the response until the subject is dropped).
- I don't discuss X anymore.

---

121. Sharon Strand Ellison, *Taking the War Out of Our Words: The Art of Powerful Non-Defensive Communication* (Berkeley: Bay Tree Publishing, 2002), 52.
122. Forward, 2013, 200.
123. Forward, 2013, 200.

- You don't have to agree with me.
- That's not up to you to decide.
- I will not discuss this with you.
- I accept that this is how you feel.

How does your communication change (or do you imagine it could change) when you speak without trying to convince, justify or over-explain your position?

What frees up inside when you are no longer beholden to trying to change her mind or get her to see things from your perspective?

Using defensive communication is kind of like panicking in quicksand. The more you panic and try to escape, the more you get sucked in. When you're panicked and reactive, you're less likely to get your point across. When dealing with a narcissist, the best thing you can do is return to the fundamental truth that you are not going to change them. Nor do you need to justify yourself either. Remember, your mother is not healthy enough to have an insightful conversation in which you express a feeling and a need and she responds with acceptance and generosity. More than likely, a typical conversation with her will aggravate and cause familiar insecurities and anxieties to arise. It's important that you not give in to the temptation to engage in passive aggressive communication, as that will just take you further into frustration. However, it does mean that having a conversation with your mother is going to look different from the way you converse with someone capable of having healthy conversations.

To go deeper, when your mother throws insults at you, belittles and condemns you, instead of reacting with arrows, simply hold up your protective shield and respond with naming your rights and your boundaries back to her—"I won't be having this conversation with you if you continue to insult me"—and exit the situation completely if she continues.

The point is not to get into a battle with her, because her narcissism is cunning and it will go to great lengths to "win." This is not a problem, because you are not here to win, though you may want to. You are only responsible for taking care of yourself in the way you see fit in that moment. You may *want* to lash out with insults, tell her off, and show her how wrong she is, but I can promise you that will not offer you any relief in a meaningful way. When we talk about taking care of yourself, we are really saying that your integrity is in your own hands. She doesn't get to determine whether or not you stay in the conversation or put up with her abuse: you do. You are in control of your behaviors, not her.

Chapter 9

THE DECISION TO GO NO-CONTACT

"I have this knack for killing plants. I don't know what it is about me, but for some reason I can't get my shit together and figure it out!" Alice shared one afternoon. Alice had been working with me for six months and we had done a lot of work around freeing up her feelings and empowering her to speak honestly in her relationships. On this day, Alice continued to explore her relationship with her mother.

As Alice shared her plight with plants, I was struck by my own thought, "This is an interesting segue." A moment before, we were talking about her relationship with her mother and how it was killing her, and now about her plants. Sometimes the unconscious mind reveals itself to us in the most fascinating ways. Ever so subtle, Alice's unconscious mind revealed a path for us to travel down, inviting us closer to understanding what Alice was not yet aware of.

"So, it doesn't quite matter what you do, the plants you house just don't make it?" I asked.

"Right. Jeff (her husband) told me that I really need to do the plants a favor and stop adopting them into our house of horrors," she laughed, revealing how fruitless and frustrating it was for her to keep experiencing the same disappointment over and over. Interesting.

I chuckled along with her, commenting that Jeff did have a point.

A pause filled the room and I asked, "Alice, did you notice what happened there? We were talking about how your relationship with your mom is killing you and your mind brought you to your plants not being able to thrive in your home. I wonder what kind of connection you are seeing there?"

Alice had tears in her eyes and was keeping her head tilted towards the floor. "I'm realizing that I can't maintain a relationship with my mom. I think I have to go no-contact." A huge sigh left her body and Alice began to weep.

Moments later Alice said, "No matter what I do, how I try with her, I end up feeling so beaten down, devalued, and psychologically broken. It's not safe or healthy for me to be in a relationship with her anymore. I'm terrified of ending it, but I know it's the only way for me to move forward in my life." I couldn't agree with her more. Just like her plants, she was not being nurtured in the way that she needed, and every interaction was like a drop of poison in the soil. Alice's inner self was expressing to her that the time had come.

"Alice, I think what you're saying is so valid and true. You've made so many strides in your healing, and this awareness comes from a deep inner wisdom. Many adult women have been in your shoes before. This is an incredibly painful part of the process. You're likely swimming in so many emotions right now, all of which are completely valid. Can you tell me how it is to share this with me?"

Alice revealed that she was feeling grief, and stated, "It's weird. I don't feel resistant to the grief. In a way, I'm recognizing that my grief is leading me toward reconciling the loss of my mother, even though she's not dead. Honestly, the clarity I'm witnessing is offering me so much relief. I can sense a feeling of liberation."

The In-Between: When You Can't Stay, but Leaving Feels Devastating

Make your relationship with your narcissistic parent your *choice* rather than your obligation. Daughters of narcissistic mothers commonly get stuck between a sense of loyalty and a desire to be completely rid of the relationship. As you embark on your recovery, it's important to be conscious of this split. The part of you that feels you must remain loyal may be the part that was raised to disavow your own needs and uphold the "rules" of family, even when that family caused harm. The part of you that wants to leave likely recognizes the benefit of this, but gets submerged by guilt and a fear of being seen unfavorably.

Let's explore for a moment some of the possible entrenched beliefs that come up alongside the "loyalty" narrative:

- What does it mean to be loyal to my mother?
- What are the costs of maintaining loyalty?
- Where did I learn about loyalty and how was that reinforced in my life?
- If I were completely free of "rules" regarding my relationship my mother, and could respond to my needs, what would that look like? How would it change my actions now?

To challenge some of the "loyalty" beliefs, let's go a step further.

The definition of *loyal* per the *Oxford Dictionary* is "giving or showing firm and constant support or allegiance to a person or institution."[124]

◗ REFLECTION

When I give my allegiance and constant support to my mother, what impact does this have on me?

If a good friend of mine were going through this exact thing, fretting about being "disloyal" if she cut ties with her narcissistic mother, what would I tell her?

----

124. *Oxford English Dictionary,* "Loyal."

Would I advise anyone else to show constant support or allegiance to a person or institution that was causing harm to them, or does this apply only to me?

Let's just notice together that when you begin to consider changing your relationship to your narcissistic mother, a familiar force pulls you back in. In some ways, you can get caught up between two extremes: either stay "loyal" or cut off contact completely. In many cases, it is necessary to engage the latter, as having a relationship with a narcissistic parent often goes nowhere and becomes an avenue for re-traumatization. However, if you are feeling truly stuck between two poles and want the option to find a middle ground, know that it's there for you.

For some daughters, going through different stages of contact is the right move. For others, going straight toward no contact is the only move to make. Recovery is not a one-size-fits-all kind of deal. Whether or not you're wanting to go through different stages of contact or cut it off entirely, it may be useful to consider some of the stages of contact in a relationship with a narcissistic mother.

1. Being loyal. Just gritting my teeth and bearing the relationship.

2. Recognizing that I need boundaries. Beginning to set limits on how I spend my time with mom. This creates a mixture of guilt and hope. The guilt is the old programming about what family means (this type of programming will say "family first" no matter what and is highly dangerous for those in abusive, toxic, and enmeshed family systems). The hope is that perhaps you can have some kind of relationship with your mother.

3. Mom becomes volatile, blaming me for the relationship "failure" and using some of her familiar tactics: veiled threats, withdrawal, becoming the victim, accusation, name-calling, long-winded texts or emails, getting mad and then becoming sweet, reminding me that I don't know what I'm doing and need her, or telling me that I'm the one with the problem. These tactics stir up feelings of anger, guilt, anxiety, and confusion. I talk to my therapist about this and I'm reminded that this is typical narcissistic behavior

that has *nothing to do with me*. This lets me take a breath and feel confident that I don't need to engage with my mom right now.

4. Strengthening my boundaries to include when I will and will not engage with mom; whether it's an in-person or over-the-phone relationship; allowing myself to go longer periods of time without engagement; telling her what she can and cannot say to me. The guilt is lessening. This inspires hope, courage, and more resilience.

5. Mom protests, but I feel better about my boundaries. I remember that it's healthy to have needs and I'm protecting myself from abusive and toxic behavior.

6. Recognizing that mom is not going to change and coming to terms with the fact that it's too painful for me to have a relationship with her in any capacity. Exploring no-contact. I begin to talk to my therapist about strengthening my resolve to do what's right for me.

In all of these stages (except the first and last one), there is the possibility that you can have what Susan Forward calls a "tea party" relationship,[125] which means it's superficial enough to allow for polite or neutral conversation, and you can report on things like how the kids are doing, what new recipe you're trying out, the latest movie you saw, or book you're reading, and can ask questions about your mother's hobbies. What you don't bring up here are your deeper feelings about your life and your struggles, as these can often be fodder for criticism and create an opening for your mother to pounce on you when you're feeling most vulnerable.

When it's time to cut the cord:

One of the most painful and laborious decisions an adult daughter can make is one that asks her to decide if she can be in relationship with her mother at all. Typically, this choice comes to a head after all else fails, and even then, there can be a lingering sense of doubt that leaves adult daughters feeling conflicted and alone. What I'd like to remind any of you who are at this crossroads is that you have tried all that you can and for your wellbeing to prevail, a path must be chosen. The path of no-contact will not be easy at first, but it will get better. The dense wood that you are currently in will open to a wide and flowering meadow where you'll have more room to grow and more space to heal.

The grief you feel from making this decision is not signifying that you are doing something wrong. Rather, it's reminding you of the reality that has been there since day one: the loss of a mother. As a child, you couldn't face this fact without suffering severe psychological distress, and, in an act of self-protection, you made your mother's flaws mean something about you. This gave you a false sense of hope, but it was hope nonetheless. As we've discussed, when children make their mother's behaviors about them, this offers a sense of control

125. Forward, *Mothers Who Can't Love*, 238

and a solution: be a "better" daughter. The grief you feel in this moment is reflecting the reality right back at you: You cannot be a "better" daughter because you were never a "bad" daughter to begin with. Your mother's narcissism is the barrier against a real and loving connection. It severs you from closeness. Your grief is the most honest ally you have, as it's showing you where you've been tied to a fantasy that cannot come to be.

Adult daughters who are contemplating going no-contact have tried everything. They've set their boundaries, expressed their needs, built a relationship to their emotions, and worked incredibly hard to be as separate from their mothers as possible. Despite all of this, their mothers continue to harass, diminish, and demean them with stunning precision. The feeling of being exposed to a narcissist is akin to having a body that is highly allergic to dairy or peanuts. This body may take in high-quality foods and plenty of water, but as soon as the allergen is ingested, smelled, or touched, the body retaliates. This body needs to have no contact with what makes it sick. You may need to make this decision regarding your mother too. It may just save your life. Even though she's still here, in some ways your mother has already left you.

▶ REFLECTION

What are you most afraid of when it comes to going no-contact?

....

....

....

....

In what way has this feared outcome already happened?

....

....

....

....

What would your life look like without her in it?

....

....

....

....

What part of your healing is being held back by keeping her in your life?

....

....

....

....

If you find yourself being consumed by a sense of guilt and fear that your actions are selfish, pause and inform this part of you that you have already tried everything; that this decision to go no-contact is for your own wellbeing. What you think of as selfish, I think of as self-respecting. Words like selfish got used against you when you were self-advocating. Remember this. Guilt was used to pull you out of taking care of yourself. This act may be necessary and vital to your wellbeing.

Bethany Webster, in her book *Discovering the Inner Mother: A Guide to Healing the Mother Wound and Claiming Your Personal Power*, writes: "Women who feel no choice but to go no-contact with their dysfunctional mothers create the break because it's the only way to send the powerful message that 'mother, your life is your own responsibility as my life is mine. I refuse to be sacrificed on the altar of your pain. I refuse to be a casualty of your war. Even though you are incapable of understanding me, I must go my own way. I must choose to truly live.'"[126]

Consider the ways in which letting this relationship go offers you a path toward greater freedom and wellbeing. Remember that although this decision is painful, it doesn't mean you are alone. From this place of death (letting mom go) and rebirth (rebuilding you), you are given an opportunity to create a new family. Starting with your own spouse/partner(s)

---

126. Webster, *Discovering the Inner Mother*, 154.

and children, and extending out to your friendships and wider community, you are nurturing a new kind of family bond into existence.

Going no-contact is not a rejection of your mother. It may feel like one, but what feels like a rejection is in actuality a decision to choose yourself. In non-narcissistic relationships, things like expressing our boundaries and talking honestly about our feelings usually lead to a deeper connection. In these relationships, mutuality and respect are the bedrock where all individuals can be heard and honored. You are not rejecting your mother. You are making yourself a priority and recognizing that your mother will never be able to show up in the way you need her to. You aren't leaving her behind, but you are leaving the system that keeps you in emotional captivity with your mother. You are leaving the toxic narrative that says, "but she's your mother" and making room for both of you to find your own way. The truth is that she will not transform into the mother you always needed her to be. Your inner child is waiting for her mother to wake up and run to her with open arms, wrapping her in an embrace that signals the end of her long and painful absence. In this reunion fantasy, your inner child hopes for her mother to finally see and accept her for who she is, reveling in her uniqueness and championing her feelings. This may be part of the reason why you've stayed in relationship to her. We are always longing for our mothers to accept us for who we are, yet narcissism robs both mother and child of that possibility. When you can finally accept this, allowing your grief, sadness, and anger to come and go, you let go of a pattern of self-constriction and open to a world of new possibilities.

Chapter 10

LIFE AFTER MOM

There is a life that exists beyond your relationship with your mother. Whether you have decided to go no-contact or maintain contact, it's important that you begin to build your life outside of your mother-daughter relationship. Healing from narcissistic abuse takes time and a lot of energy, and it's not uncommon to forget that you have other aspirations and dreams in your life. Many of the women I've worked with have put extensive work into separating themselves from their mothers. These women have fought tooth and nail to reclaim what was stolen from them in their childhood so that they can feel whole again. It's so important that as you do this work, you cultivate a life that is entirely your own, separate from your mother and open to all kinds of new possibilities.

Toko-pa Turner, author, mystic, and dreamworker, writes extensively about the notion of belonging. In her book *Belonging: Remembering Ourselves Home*, Turner explores the art of learning to belong to ourselves, reminding the reader that we can be a container unto ourselves in which all parts of who we are belong. This chapter is dedicated to the practice of belonging; of taking all parts of the self that have had to be shut out and left to survive on their own, and reuniting them in their rightful place, which is within us.

In my mind, belonging starts from a place of compassion. From this place, we turn toward the parts of us that have felt unworthy or bad and telling them, "I'm so sorry I ever thought you didn't belong." Say these words to your fiery anger, the deep grief within your bones, your messiness, the wild and carefree energy that lets you play, your imagination that took you to other worlds, and to your exquisite sensitivity. All of these parts are worthy participants in your life; without them you live only a half-life.

In Turner's book, much of her emphasis is on remembering ourselves home. What does it mean to remember yourself home? What image comes to your mind when you read this phrase? What do you notice happening in your body?

When we are remembering, we are bringing something to mind by either calling something up from a past place or by attempting to retain something we just learned. In remembering ourselves home, we are also tasked with re-memorying. When you look upon your past experiences, you may be doing so from the perspective of the child you once were. However, as you reflect on your past, please do so from the perspective of your adult self, who is in a different time and place. This is where you can re-memory the experience with new information that was not available to you as a child.

Take a moment to come back into your body and mind right now. Let's get to know this adult self that exists outside of your mother. Can you describe her as a three-dimensional being with values, complex feelings, shadow parts, and aspirations? Does she enjoy laughing with the fullness of her belly in one instance and in the next nestling into sweet solitude? When she is operating from a place of inner freedom, does she permit herself to notice and dive into her desires? When she needs respite from the bustling of her life, does she seek out those quiet spaces to reclaim her energy? Are her relationships formed from a place of honesty and mutual respect? Can she express herself organically and with integrity to others in her life?

Staying connected to ourselves requires that we be willing to notice what we're feeling and experiencing moment to moment. Of course, this is not about achieving perfect presence, but more about the willingness to tune in when we notice ourselves drifting away. Throughout this book you have seen a distinction made between your child and adult selves. Now, we are exploring the idea of the adult self making room for the inner child that was neglected. The inner child is now looking to the adult self for guidance and care. As you continue to come back to your feelings and needs with interest, the inner child feels a sense a belonging.

In this moment, do you notice any part of you that is calling out for some care and attention? What would this part most love to hear or experience right now? If you're unable to respond to this part or give it what it needs, can you make that known? It's amazing how simply acknowledging parts of ourselves is healing in and of itself.

Belonging

What does it mean to belong?

Belonging isn't a place, but a skill.[127] It is a practice of allowing all parts of ourselves to dare to belong and be cared for. When we allow all parts of us to belong, we become a healing container where metamorphosis is possible. I like to think of this practice as offering a place of warmth to the parts of ourselves that have been left behind in the cold. These travelers within us sigh with great relief at the sight of refuge awaiting.

When narcissistic mothers cut the umbilical cord of connection, daughters must find sustenance within. That doesn't come easy. Without the life-giving nourishment from our mothers, we become like vultures taking what we can get, hungrily awaiting the next dead thing. The way out of this deprived state is to know what we're looking for and offer it to ourselves. In her book, Turner writes that "if you can stand fully in your own unbelonging and become friendly with the terrors of loneliness and exclusion, you can no longer be governed by your avoidance of them. In other words, you are on your way home."[128]

From Survival Self to Real Self

As you embark on moving forward and living your life, you'll naturally want to feel more like you are living from an authentic self. How do we get there? It's important to first recognize that in your life, you had to develop a survival self. The survival self will allow you to display only the traits that were considered acceptable and hides the parts that were ridiculed, ignored, or humiliated. These rejected parts are like refugees that must be kept unseen by tyrannical forces. After so many instances of self-hiding, a kind of normalcy sets in where this survival self becomes the standard.

If you've lived in a place that once was full of trees and nature only to return and see it developed into a concrete jungle, you'll eventually forget the wildness that came before it. Here, we must help you re-wild back to your authentic nature. This authentic self contains all of the realness that comes with being human. Much like an ecosystem, all parts and feelings are needed to support the whole. When one part of an ecosystem gets threatened, it stymies the natural flow between each organism, which eventually devastates the entire system. Your ecosystem was subjected to the interference of a toxic invader: Narcissism. To recuperate, it's important that you allow your natural feelings to flow freely so that you can

---

127. Toko-pa Turner, *Belonging: Remembering Ourselves Home* (British Columbia: Her Own Room Press, 2017), 16.
128. Turner, *Belonging*, 21.

feel whole again. As you stand by your own side, you are forever accompanied and your inner system can return to its natural state.

Adult daughters have learned to play the role of "nice girl" and "people pleaser." Let rebellion be a passenger on your return home to yourself. In what ways have you laid yourself down in front of your narcissistic mother? This reflection should be without judgment aimed at yourself, but with a willingness to recognize how you had to surrender so much in order to survive. As children or dependents, we make ourselves small when we have no other way of escaping or fighting back. As adults who are unlearning where we may still be complicit in our own neglect, we must learn new ways to self-protect that feel more like standing tall, taking up space, and using our voices.

Where we can wrest control back into our own hands lies in how we attend to ourselves. If you can approach each part of you with a sense of welcome and interest, then you have broken a cycle of trauma. When you open the door and invite each part of you in, there lies an opportunity for self-growth and transformation.

However, we may not yet feel welcoming toward every part of ourselves. The pain, anger, shame, and fear may feel all too overwhelming, and the temptation to slam the door in their faces is high. Those unrecognized emotions may have felt like alarm bells going off, alerting you to the possibility of being exiled from the family tribe. But it is through exile that we find ourselves.[129] The journey that we take out of an established tribe often reveals the parts of ourselves that have been living as outcasts. Put another way, we must confront the parts of ourselves that have been dormant while we survived. On the experience of exile, Turner writes, "Then there is a quest or journey put before her, which she must undertake to find her true place in the world. But to do so she must leave home, breaking from her established group or family, to endure a long period of exile."[130]

True Belonging

In another book on belonging, *Braving the Wilderness: The Quest for True Belonging and the Courage to Stand Alone*, the inimitable Brené Brown describes the practice of True Belonging as a willingness to stand alone and risk being authentic and true to ourselves, knowing that it may leave us alone in the end. But the thing is, you are never alone when you belong to yourself. And being true to ourselves is a practice that at times can be as terrifying as it is wonderful and enlightening. The process of true belonging is akin to never

---

129. Turner, *Belonging*, 70.
130. Turner, *Belonging*, 29.

again abandoning who you are in favor of fitting in. When you belong to yourself, you are free.

In *Braving the Wilderness*, Brown defines True Belonging as "the spiritual practice of believing in and belonging to yourself so deeply that you can share your most authentic self with the world and find sacredness in both being a part of something and standing alone in the wilderness. True belonging doesn't require you to change who you are; it requires you to *be* who you are."[131]

Brown writes that the path out of loneliness and back into true belonging is through choosing courage over comfort. She states that "belonging to ourselves means sometimes having to find the courage to stand alone, totally alone."[132] We do this by forging a connection to our inner explorer that can take us into new and exciting vistas. Our path into authenticity is not without fear. Anytime we journey into uncharted territory we are likely to feel fear and uncertainty, among other feelings. If we stop and examine what the fear is, we might discover old remnants from our former lives as children. Beliefs that come from early childhood may sound like:

- "If I stand out, I'll get picked on."
- "It's better to keep the peace than risk chaos."
- "If I say what I feel, I'll get abandoned."
- "My parents (other people) won't know how to deal with me if I say what I feel."
- "I'll just be ridiculed."

As you can see, flecks of shame and the fear of not belonging are woven deep into these beliefs. We are all of us wired to connect with our tribe, and any threat of disconnection (i.e., vulnerability or having opinions and beliefs that are different from those of the group) gets coded as a threat to *survival*. Our need to fit in feels like life or death. The problem is that when we sacrifice our authentic selves in favor of fitting in, we end up feeling more like strangers to ourselves and, ironically, disconnected from others. Trying to fit in actually creates more loneliness. The way out of this is to make the commitment to belong to ourselves, which will feel very different from fitting in. Your authentic self is waiting for you. Reclaiming the aspects of ourselves that were discarded and rejected, and inviting them to have a seat at the table, is what reunites us with our core selves and invites us into true belonging.

---

131. Brené Brown, *Braving the Wilderness: The Quest for True Belonging and the Courage to Stand Alone* (New York: Random House, 2019), 40.

132. Brown, *Braving the Wilderness,* 32.

Be hospitable toward all parts of yourself. Allow them to visit, to have a place by the fire where they can tell you their truth. When core feelings like rage, joy, care, lust, fear, and disgust all have a place to belong within yourself, then there's no need to waste energy pushing them away. Energy that once went into avoidance, numbing, withdrawal, or rumination can now be put back into yourself in the form of awareness, caring, and nurturance.

◐ EXERCISE: RECLAIMING YOUR DISCARDED SELVES

As an exercise, I'd like for you to take a moment to write out a list of all the parts of yourself that you have learned to judge and see as unattractive, wrong, or problematic. List these parts on a piece of paper. Next, I'd like for you to imagine these parts as living beings. When these living beings are told that they are wrong and unworthy of inclusion, how do you imagine they respond? Write out their reactions. Do these living beings simply vanish when they are given their sentence of exile? Where do they go?

On another page, I'd like you to rewrite the parts of you that have been excluded and exiled. Next to them, ask the question: "Would you like a place to belong again?" Write out the answers.

Last, I'd like for you to ask these parts, "How would you like to be treated from now on?" Listen. Stay with any silences that arise and keep listening. How would these parts like to belong to you? Would they like understanding, inclusion, and some acceptance? How would it feel for you to offer this to them?

Gwen

Gwen shared with me how terrified she was of other people judging her. This could be anyone from romantic partners to coworkers, bosses, and her therapist (me). Outside of her mother's judgment, she hadn't experienced anyone directly judging her, but despite this reality, Gwen found herself reacting to everyone as though they were judging. This set her up to fail in two ways: 1) she would either become incredibly angry toward someone, believing that they were secretly judging or ridiculing her in their mind, or 2) she'd go quiet and become fearful that whomever she was with would not only judge, but abandon her. In either direction, Gwen found herself relating to individuals based on her own past experiences rather than what was occurring in the moment.

One session we explored how she deals with her fears of judgment and abandonment from others.

"I tend to either explode or shrink into myself. It sucks. When I lash out, I instantly feel guilty, and guess what? They do end up judging me. I even ended a relationship once because I was convinced that they were going to leave me, which is just so painfully ironic, right?"

Gwen was acutely aware that, without meaning to, she would incite the judgment of others, and as you can see above, create the thing she was afraid of. Gwen came to realize that her big fears came from early childhood experiences where her mother would use the threat of abandonment to manipulate and scare Gwen out of her feelings. Her mother's outbursts threatened Gwen's sense of safety, so she did what any child would do: catered to her mother's needs in order to prevent being deserted.

As an adult, continuing to use the strategy of a seven-year-old no longer made sense. It enraged her to have to put so much of her self-energy into the needs of her partner, friends, and family members. To combat this, she would lash out, unconsciously taking on her mother's role in her own life. Only this time it served her in a self-defeating way, and the thing she feared became the thing she created.

As Gwen began to see these entrenched patterns, she started to make newer choices. Her lifelong habit of either lashing out or shrinking began to disperse to the point where she could make room for newer responses. Within that space, she started to register just how often she was left alone with a lot of fear as a child. This generated enormous compassion for her child self. Now, when she turned toward her fear and greeted it as a guest, she recognized that it was coming from an old memory from the past, rather than from something happening now. Gwen told me that in the past, her fear would completely envelop her to where she was living from it, rather than seeing it as a feeling state she could be curious about.

Survival Self Part Two

A while ago, we talked about how you had to develop a survival self to preserve your relationship with your mother and other caregivers. Your survival self developed out of an ingenious attempt at keeping you safe. Whatever you used to survive then, however, has a shelf life. Just like a baby no longer needs a rattle to self-soothe, or a favorite stuffed animal to help them sleep, it is time for you to outgrow that which you no longer need. These survival strategies worked perfectly as a child, but they are not needed in this place and time.

BREAK FREE FROM NARCISSISTIC MOTHERS

What do you need to let go of in order to grow something new? The weeds that kept your tender flower bed concealed must be uprooted so that the seeds you sow now can finally bloom. When the overgrowth has been pruned, what parts of yourself are waiting to blossom? Do you have forgotten parts of yourself that are longing to spring out from the soil? What are the seeds of your authentic self that you'd like to bring into being?

As a child, you took on a role in your mother's story. Never knowing you could be a sovereign self, you became an extension of her. There was no space for you to listen to your own body's wisdom or calls to action for your life's purpose. Now, as you piece together the lost parts of yourself, you'll see a beautiful tapestry that is calling for your attention, as it always did. This tapestry belongs to you. The broken pieces of your mother are not your responsibility to heal, nor are they yours to hold onto. You and your mother must be separate now. Your hidden self must break free and be allowed to move about in the world, unrestricted. In her book *Mother-Daughter Wisdom*, Christiane Northrup writes that "every woman who heals herself helps heal all the women who came before her and all those who will come after her."[133]

Should I Forgive My Mom?

It is a misconception to suggest that forgiveness is the only way to truly heal. Daughters who have been influenced by forgiveness culture may think that if they don't do this "final step" in their recovery, they will not be fully healed. I'd like to gently call bullshit on that.

Our culture likes to promote the notion that forgiveness is the final step needed for emotional healing. Even within the world of psychology, forgiveness is touted as a sign of one's evolution in letting the past go. Forgiveness can be a wonderful act that, when felt deeply, makes way for something new and transformational. There are plenty of religious communities who make forgiveness a practice, which for some offers a nourishing pathway toward a lightened spirit. Where forgiveness becomes problematic is when it is touted as a condition of "moving on," or seen as a choice that you must eventually make to heal. Here's the thing: *sometimes forgiveness is impossible. And that's okay.*

Have you felt the pressure to forgive your mom in some way, but try as you might, cannot get there? This is not a failure on your part, not a sign of your ""badness," certainly not required in order for you to heal. Many well-intentioned individuals miss the mark when it comes to preaching forgiveness.

---

133. Christiane Northrup, *Mother-Daughter Wisdom: Understanding the Crucial Link between Mothers, Daughters, and Health* (New York: Bantam Dell, 2006), 3.

While forgiveness as a whole can be a deeply healing and monumental experience for the one giving and the one receiving *in some cases*, it is not a cure-all, nor should it be treated as the one golden path forward. A foundational belief system that permeates my practice is the complete and total acceptance of an individual's decision *not* to forgive their narcissistic mother or *need* to do so in order to move on. There are many schools of thought about the virtues of forgiveness and I encourage you to explore them if you wish. However, at the end of the day it is entirely your choice. No one has the right to tell you to forgive or not to forgive. That is your choice.

I will not boast any dogmatic stance on forgiveness. There is no right path in either direction, forgiveness or not. Attempting to be black and white with these very personal choices only creates more suffering in the end. Allow yourself to the freedom to do *what is best for you*. However, if you are struggling with the concept of forgiveness because you feel you *should* in order to move forward in your life, I want to gently stop you and let you know that it is not necessary. Nor is it required of you in order to reach some next level in your healing. And at the same time, forgiveness is yours if you wish to strive for it.

If forgiveness is something you feel you should get to but can't, I'd like for you to stop and journal out some of your thoughts driving the "should." Here are a few prompts to get you started.

◗ REFLECTION

What is motivating you to wish to forgive your mother?

What steps have you taken to move in this direction? Have they helped?

If forgiveness were not mandatory for you to heal, what would you be striving for now?

....

....

....

How do you treat yourself when you cannot feel forgiveness? Would you say this self-treatment empowers or disempowers you?

....

....

....

What do you imagine would happen if you did forgive your mother?

....

....

....

If you had a child and someone treated them the way your mother treated you, would you demand they forgive that person one day? How would you feel if they didn't want to?

....

....

....

Is the response you'd give to your child empowering or disempowering?

Can you consider forgiving yourself for not being able to forgive? If you can't do that, you're not ready for forgiveness anyway (and you don't need to be, either).

I have seen so many adult daughters struggle with this. My hope is that you can start to realize that forgiveness is not the only path toward healing. Many adult daughters recover from the effects of maternal narcissism without needing to forgive. In fact, most find their healing through self-acceptance, a practice that embraces all parts of the self as welcomed guests. Forgiveness is a very nuanced construct that should not be taken lightly. When we cannot forgive, it is not because we are choosing hate or choosing resentment. Rather, we are honoring the part of us that was wounded and abused and standing by her side, trusting that our healthy anger will continue to uphold our boundaries. You do not have to let the past go in order to be free. When we're in *relationship to ourselves*, we know what is right for us. No one can tell you how to feel or what your relationship to your mother "should" look like. *Should* doesn't get a place here. *Should* can be reserved for questions like "what should we have for dinner? Should I wear the blue or red dress? Should we go to skiing this year?" Not "you should really get over that now." Our experiences are our own and no one is entitled to tell us how to relate to them.

For those of you who are seeking forgiveness out of a genuine desire (i.e., you are not feeling pressured to do this), then you've won half the battle. The next steps are for you to really get in touch with the why behind your choice.

◖ REFLECTION

What value, belief, or desire is motivating you to do this?

....

....

....

How does it feel inside when you connect with this decision?

....

....

....

Does forgiveness include you too? If not, why? If so, tell me more about that. Let's get to know that why too.

....

....

....

What would forgiving your mother offer you? What makes this most important for you?

....

....

....

Forgiveness, in my opinion, can be done after we've fully allowed ourselves the opportunity to feel as deeply as we need to about our past. Do not feel obligated in any way to offer forgiveness to an abusive, toxic or neglectful mother who cannot recognize her own cruelty. It is highly unlikely that she will own up to her behavior or recognize that she contributed to your pain. When we are pushed to forgive those who have caused us significant pain, it feeds the belief system that we must "rise above" and behave like saints. This is not only harmful, but unrealistic. You'll know you've stepped into this toxic place when you feel guilt, shame, and a kind of inner tension take over. Please note, by stating the above I am not suggesting you *never* strive for forgiveness or find a way to make peace with your mother; however, I do wish to caution you against prematurely moving toward something that is neither required of you nor necessary for healing.

True healing can be ushered in when we stand with the parts of ourselves that were bullied, shamed, abused, neglected, or harmed and refuse to ignore them any further. By taking this caring stance toward ourselves, we then have more freedom to make authentic choices about how we want to move forward in our relationships. You may discover that standing by these abused parts of yourself means holding them with complete acceptance for what they need and require. These angry and scared parts may never want to forgive and should not be forced to comply with an arbitrary "rule" of recovery.

However, you may also discover the complete opposite. By holding space for your pain and humiliation, you may discover a newfound capacity to do the same for your mother and what she experienced as a child, which necessitated her narcissistic defense. Most narcissistic mothers were also raised by narcissistic parents or abusive caregivers. This caring presence for yourself could extend to your mother and foster a kind of forgiveness and compassion that can witness both your and your mother's trauma.

Narcissists operate with a very limited battery life. Their drive to get away from their own shame and sense of unworthiness is an unconscious force that motivates their behavior. This is what leads them to become grandiose narcissists or covert, where they act the part of the self-sacrificing martyr/victim. From a distance, one might feel compassion for these deeply troubled individuals who will never feel good enough. However, while this may be doable for a person on the outside looking in, it may be nearly impossible for you, the daughter of a narcissist, to do the same.

If you can feel compassion for your mother, I hope you feel it equally toward yourself, and if you can't, I hope you can get curious as to why. Self-compassion is the wellspring from which we all must draw in order to feel compassion for others. We cannot truly experience the depth of what compassion offers without holding that same care for ourselves. However, here we are talking about recovering from narcissistic abuse, and there is a fine line between toxic and healthy compassion, just as there is a toxic and healthy form of forgiveness in this work.

The real person who ought to be seeking forgiveness is your mother. However, even if she does seek it, it does not mean you must offer it. Real atonement must be expressed specifically, in detail, where the individual recognizes exactly what they did, and how and why it hurt you, and commits to making it right. The person seeking real forgiveness should also be at a place where they can truly accept *not* receiving it. They don't expect forgiveness, nor are they demanding of it. There's a real "open arms" stance they take, which conveys: "I did something wrong. I want to make it right. I accept if you cannot forgive me and will not require it of you. Regardless, I am committed to changing my behavior."

Narcissistic mothers can't offer forgiveness if they are bound by the constraints and false-hoods of their narcissism. To forgive, they would sincerely need to be able to see their actions from your perspective, and most narcissists cannot do that without it feeling like a threat to their sense of self. What makes narcissists so difficult to penetrate is their belief that says "I am right and you are wrong," which makes seeking forgiveness from them nearly impossible.

Caring for Your Inner Child

Healing is never a done thing, but a lifelong practice. Like a spiral staircase, we travel through many winding steps, sometimes continuing up and other times needing to travel back down. The part of us that can witness our pain from a place of nonjudgmental awareness is always present. This part is like the observer of our lives, benevolent and unaffected by the world around us. No person, emotion, or situation will ever scare this part of us away. This higher, larger self is our godlike nature. Like a constant presence, it allows us to see truth. You will always have this higher self to tap into. In this way, you are never alone.

The pain you've experienced from your childhood is yours to tend to as an adult woman. It now lies in the past. The inner child who experienced that pain needs you to grieve with her, feel outraged on her behalf, and commit to standing by her side. She's there waiting for you to return to her. What she needs, you can now give to her. What she feels, you can fully embrace. Take her in where she can be fully held and supported.

BIBLIOGRAPHY

American Psychiatric Association. *Diagnostic and Statistical Manual of Mental Disorders.* 5th ed. Washington DC: American Psychiatric Association, 2013.

Ashley, Patti. *Shame-Informed Therapy: Treatment Strategies to Overcome Core Shame and Reconstruct the Authentic Self.* Eau Claire, WI: PESI Publishing & Media, 2020. Kindle.

Badt, Karin Luisa. "A Dialogue with Neuroscientist Jaak Panksepp on the SEEKING System: Breaking the Divide between Emotion and Cognition in Film Studies." *Projections* 9, no. 1 (June 2015): 66–79. https://doi.org/10.3167/proj.2015.090105.

Brach, Tara. *Radical Compassion: Learning to Love Yourself and Your World with the Practice of R.A.I.N.* New York: Penguin Random House, 2019.

Brackett, Marc. *Permission to Feel: Unlocking the Power of Emotions to Help Our Kids, Ourselves, and Our Society Thrive.* New York: Celadon Books, 2019.

Brenner, Helene. *I Know I'm in There Somewhere: A Woman's Guide to Finding Her Inner Voice and Living a Life of Authenticity.* New York: Gotham Books, 2004.

Brown, Brené. *Braving The Wilderness: The Quest for True Belonging and the Courage to Stand Alone.* New York: Random House, 2019. Kindle.

Burgo, Joseph. *Why Do I Do That?: Psychological Defense Mechanisms and the Hidden Ways They Shape Our Lives.* Chapel Hill, NC: New Rise Press, 2012. Kindle.

Butterfield, Ingrid. "The Myth of Jocasta and Maternal Narcissism." *Australasian Psychiatry* 20, no. 2 (March 2012): 153–56. https://doi.org/10.1177/1039856212438952.

Charles, Marilyn. "Stealing Beauty: An Exploration of Maternal Narcissism." *The Psychoanalytic Review* 88, no. 4 (August, 2001): 549–70. https://doi.org/10.1521/prev.88.4.549.17817.

Cramer, Phebe. "Narcissism and Attachment: The Importance of Early Parenting." *The Journal of Nervous and Mental Disease* 207, no. 2 (2019): 69–75. http://doi.org/10.1097/NMD.0000000000000919.

Dana, Deb. *Polyvagal Exercises for Safety and Connection: 50 Client-Centered Practices.*

Delaney, Kathleen R. "Following the Affect: Learning to Observe Emotional Regulation." *Journal of Child and Adolescent Psychiatric Nursing* 19, no. 4 (November, 2006): 175 – 81. https://doi.org/10.1111/j.1744-6171.2006.00069.x.

DeYoung, Patricia A. *Understanding and Treating Chronic Shame: A Relational/Neurobiological Approach.* New York: Routledge, 2015.

Dickinson, Kelly A., and Aaron L. Pincus. "Interpersonal Analysis of Grandiose and Vulnerable Narcissism." *Journal of Personality Disorders* 17, no. 3 (June, 2003): 188-207. https://doi.org/10.1521/pedi.17.3.188.22146.

Duschinsky, Robbie. "The Emergence of the Disorganized/Disoriented (D) Attachment Classification, 1979-1982." *History of Psychology* 18, no.1: 32–46. http://dx.doi.org/10.1037/a0038524.

Ehrlich, Robert. "Winnicott's Idea of The False Self: Theory as Autobiography." *Journal of the American Psychoanalytic Association* 69, no. 1 (February, 2021): 75-108. https://doi.org/10.1177/00030651211001461.

Ellison, Sharon Strand. *Taking the War Out of Our Words: The Art of Powerful Non-Defensive Communication.* Berkeley, CA: Bay Tree Publishing, 2002.

Forward, Susan. *Mothers Who Can't Love: A Healing Guide for Daughters.* New York: HarperCollins, 2013.

Hall, Julie L. *The Narcissist in Your Life: Recognizing the Patterns and Learning to Break Free.* New York: Da Capo Lifelong Books, 2019.

Harper, Faith G. *Unfuck Your Boundaries: Build Better Relationships through Consent, Communication, and Expressing Your Needs.* 2nd ed. Portland, OR: Microcosm Publishing, 2019. Kindle.

Hayes, Steven. C. *A Liberated Mind: How to Pivot Towards What Matters.* New York: Avery, 2019. Kindle.

Herbert, Frank. *Dune.* New York: Ace Publishing, 1990.

Jacobs Hendel, Hilary. *It's Not Always Depression: Working the Change Triangle to Listen to the Body, Discover Core Emotions, and Connect to Your Authentic Self.* New York: Penguin Random House, 2018. Kindle.

Katherine, Anne. *Boundaries: Where You End and I Begin—How To Recognize And Set Healthy Boundaries.* Boca Raton, FL: Parkside Publishing, 1991.

Kross, Ethan, Emma Bruehlman-Senecal, Jiyoung Park, Aleah Burson, Adrienne Dougherty, Holly Shablack, Ryan Bremner, Jason Moser, and Ozlem Ayduk. "Self-Talk as a Regulatory Mechanism: How You Do It Matters." *Journal of Personality and Social Psychology* 106, no. 2 (February, 2014): 304-24. https://doi.org/10.1037/a0035173.

Levy, Kenneth N. "Subtypes, Dimensions, Levels, and Mental States in Narcissism and Narcissistic Personality Disorder." *Journal of Clinical Psychology* 68, no. 8 (January 2012): 886-97. https://doi.org/10.1002/jclp.21893.

Levy, Kenneth N., Benjamin N. Johnson, Tracy L. Clouthier, Wesley J. Scala, and Christina M. Temes. "An Attachment Theoretical Framework for Personality Disorders." *Canadian Psychology/ Psychologie Canadienne* 56, no. 2 (May 2015): 197-207. https://doi.org/10.1037/cap0000025.

Lovenheim, Peter. *The Attachment Effect: Exploring the Powerful Ways Our Earliest Bond Shapes Our Relationships and Lives.* New York: TarcherPerigee, 2018.

Lowen, Alexander. *Narcissism: Denial of the True Self.* New York: Simon & Schuster, 1985.

Markin, Rayna D., Kevin S. McCarthy, Amy Fuhrman, Danny Yeung, and Kari A. Gleiser. "The Process of Change in Accelerated Experiential Dynamic Psychotherapy (AEDP): A Case Study Analysis." *Journal of Psychotherapy Integration* 28, no. 2 (June, 2018): 213-32. https://doi.org/10.1037/int0000084.

Martinez-Lewi, Linda. *Freeing Yourself from the Narcissist in Your Life.* New York: Penguin, 2008.

Maté, Gabor. "Compassionate Inquiry." Training Course. January 2019.

McLaren, Karla. "Welcoming the Gifts of Sadness." Accessed June 28, 2021. https://karlamclaren.com/welcoming-the-gifts-of-sadness/.

Miller, Alice. *Prisoners of Childhood: The Drama of the Gifted Child and the Search for the True Self.* New York: Basic Books, 1981.

Nerenberg, Jeanara. "Why Are So Many Adults Today Haunted by Trauma?" *Greater Good Magazine.* Last modified June 8, 2017. https://greatergood.berkeley.edu/article/item/why_are_so_many_adults_today_haunted_by_trauma.

Northrup, Christine. *Mother-Daughter Wisdom: Understanding the Crucial Link between Mothers, Daughters, and Health.* New York: Bantam Dell, 2006.

Oxford English Dictionary. 2nd ed. Oxford: Oxford University Press, 2004.

Panksepp, Jaak. "Cross-Species Affective Neuroscience Decoding of the Primal Affective Experiences of Humans and Related Animals." *PLoS ONE* 6, no. 9 (September 2011): e21236. https://doi.org/10.1371/journal.pone.0021236.

Paterson, Randy J. *The Assertiveness Workbook: How to Express Your Ideas and Stand Up for Yourself at Work and in Relationships.* Oakland: New Harbinger Publications, 2000. Kindle.

PDM Task Force. *Psychodynamic Diagnostic Manual.* Silver Spring: Alliance of Psychoanalytic Organizations, 2006, 44-46.

Peyton, Sarah. *Your Resonant Self: Guided Meditations and Exercises to Engage Your Brain's Capacity for Healing.* New York: W.W. Norton & Company, 2017. Kindle.

Pincus, Aaron L., and Mark. R. Lukowitsky. "Pathological Narcissism and Narcissistic Personality Disorder." *Annual Review of Clinical Psychology* 6 (April 2010): 421-46. https://doi.org/10.1146/annurev.clinpsy.121208.131215.

Ronningstam, Elsa. "Narcissistic Personality Disorder: A Clinical Perspective." *The Journal of Psychiatric Practice* 17, no. 2 (March 2011): 89-99. https://doi.org/10.1097/01.pra.0000396060.67150.40.

Rosenberg, Marshall. *Living Nonviolent Communication: Practical Tools to Connect and Communicate Skillfully in Every Situation.* Louisville, CO: Sounds True, Inc., 2012. Kindle.

Shaw, Daniel. *Traumatic Narcissism: Relational Systems of Subjugation.* New York: Routledge, 2013.

Turner, Toko-pa. *Belonging: Remembering Ourselves Home.* British Columbia, Canada: Her Own Room Press, 2017.

Webster, Bethany. *Discovering the Inner Mother: A Guide to Healing the Mother Wound and Claiming Your Personal Power.* New York: William Morrow and Company, 2021. Kindle.

ACKNOWLEDGMENTS

To my clients, who have taught me the true meaning of courage, resilience, and street smarts. I owe so much gratitude and thanks for the ways in which you show up and do the work. Your strength gives me strength.

I'd like to acknowledge all of the people in my life who have made a difference in my work and how I practice psychotherapy. I would like to first give my deepest gratitude to Susan Warren Warshow, LCSW, LMFT, whose groundbreaking work has influenced my approach to psychotherapy. Susan's teachings are nothing less than transformational. It is from her unflinching commitment to the human spirit that I have gleaned my own courage. I would also like to express my thanks and love to Bridget Quebodeaux, whose mentorship and guidance has elevated my confidence not only in my work, but in my life. To all of my wonderful DEFT colleagues, for being exceptional leaders and healers. To my partner in crime, my beautiful family, and friends who have been so instrumental in helping me grow and expand.

Last, I'd like to deeply thank the team at Ulysses Press for helping birth this book into existence. I am and will always be forever grateful.

ABOUT THE AUTHOR

Hannah Alderete is a licensed mental health counselor who works with adult children of narcissists to help them achieve self-acceptance through a practice known as Dynamic Emotion Focused Therapy (DEFT). As a therapist, Hannah believes that true healing comes about when we allow ourselves to feel fully, express and honor our needs, and live in accordance to our values. Outside of therapy, Hannah is an avid reader of sci-fi, fantasy, and fiction, a yogi, an animal lover, and a wannabe meditator. It is her hope to one day get her PhD in psychology and continue to grow, practice, and expand as a learner, teacher, and healer.

Nicholas Jarry